The Iceman

Third edition 2000

Translation: Isabel Naylon
Graphic Design: Gruppe Gut Graphics, Bz
Photolithography: Typestudio, Bz
Printing: La Commerciale Borgogno, Bolzano
ISBN: 3-85256-100-0

The Iceman

Angelika Fleckinger/Hubert Steiner

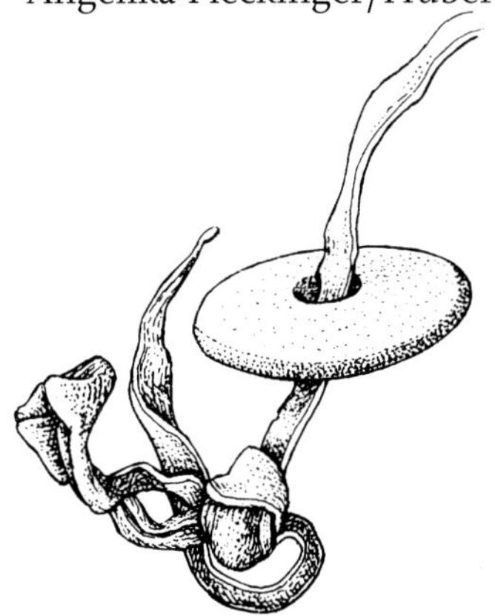

folio

Contents

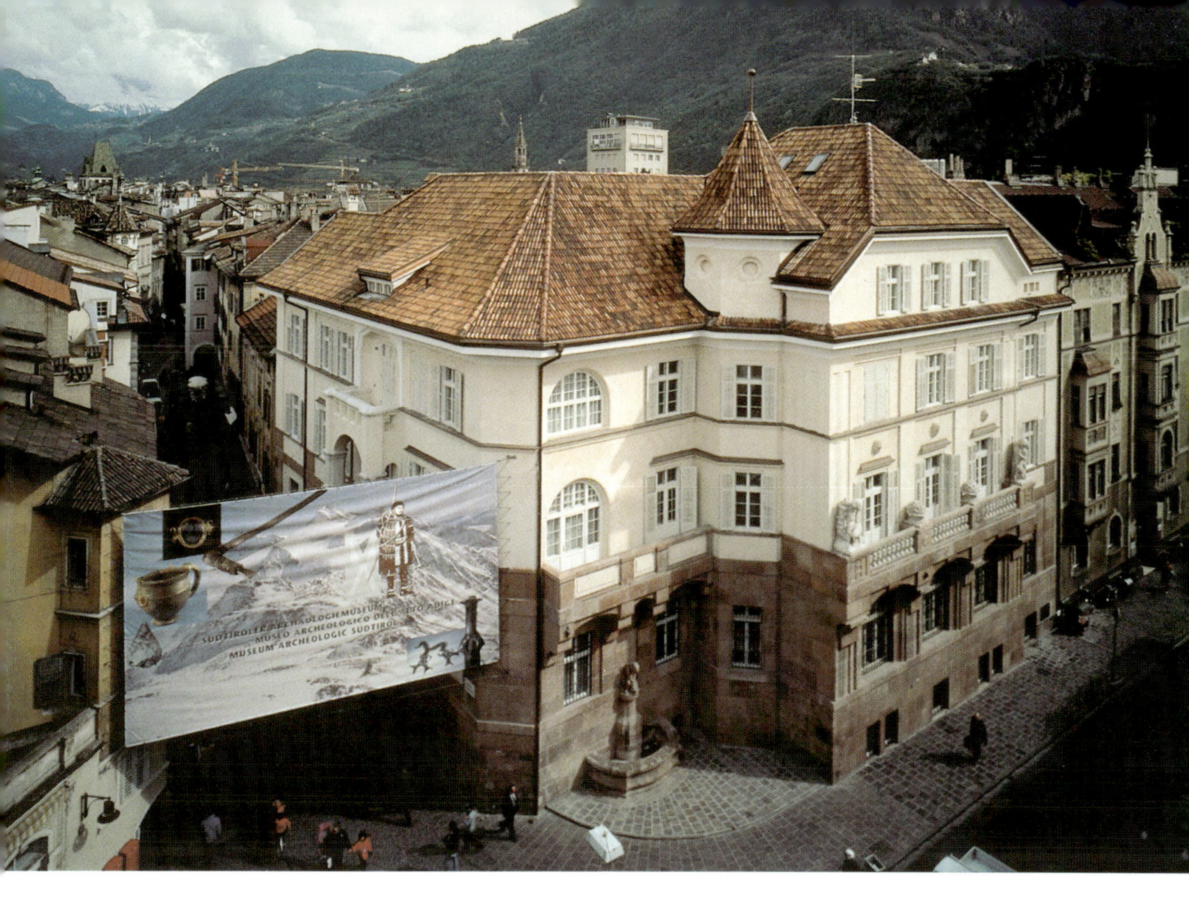
SÜDTIROLER ARCHÄOLOGIEMUSEUM
MUSEUM ARCHEOLOGIC SÜDTIROL

The Iceman

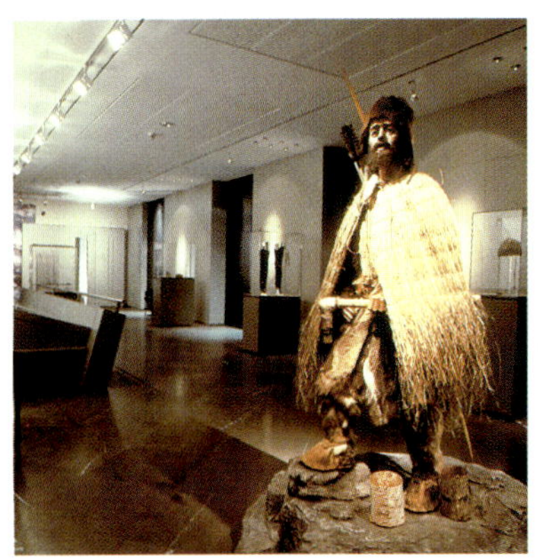

Introduction

The present catalogue includes a brief history of the Iceman from his discovery in 1991 to the exhibition of the mummy and the items found with him in the South Tyrol Museum of Archaeology.
An overview is given of all the findings and of the results of the research. The texts in the catalogue are based on the summaries of the research results provided by Markus Egg (Mainz), Walter Leitner (Innsbruck) and Konrad Spindler (Innsbruck).

The discovery

It was on Thursday 19th September 1991 that Erika and Helmut Simon, a couple from Nuremberg, left the marked mountain trail on their descent from the Finailspitze to the Similaun refuge and came upon a gully in the rock filled with glacier ice and meltwater. In this gully they discovered a corpse of which the head and part of the torso were sticking out of the ice. They documented the find with a photo. Next to the corpse the couple

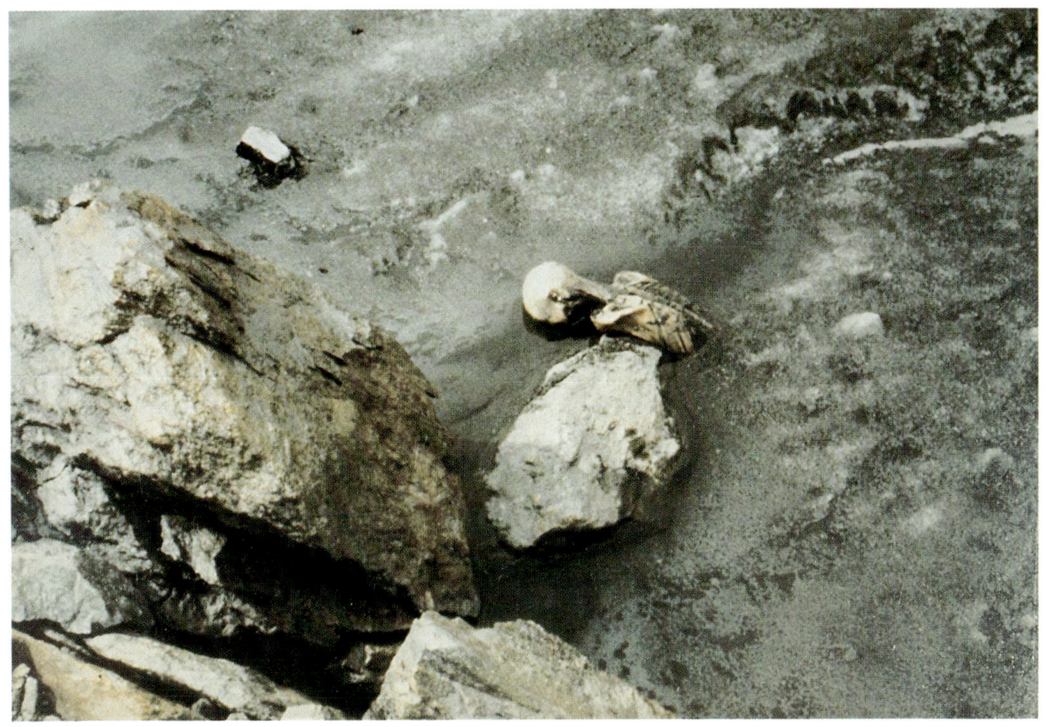

One of the first photographs of the mummy taken after the discovery

noticed the remains of a container made of birch-bark. When they arrived at the Similaun refuge they told the hut-keeper of their discovery. It was then officially reported to the carabinieri in Senales and the constabulary in Sölden.

The location of the find

The location of the find is at an altitude of 3,210 m above sea level right next to the summer trail from the Similaun refuge to the col of Tisen-joch - approximately 73 m below the latter. It is located on the edge of the Niederjochferner between the steep slope towards Senales and the flatter glacier ridge into the Niedertal towards Vent in the Ötztal. The main Alpine ridge can be crossed over three cols at this point: over the Niederjoch, over the Tisenjoch and over the Hauslabjoch. Farmers from the Senales valley still drive their sheep over the Tisenjoch and Niederjoch to the Ötztal Alpine pastures.

The Iceman was discovered in an approximately 40 m long and 5–8 m wide gully which is sunk 2.5–3 m deep into the rock. When the mummy was discovered there was still 60–80 cm of ice in the gully. The approximately 30 cm of melt water and ice drained off towards the north-east in the direction of the Niederjochferner. The topography had protected the find from the force of the ice flowing over it since the Copper Age and had thus allowed the objects to maintain more or less their original order. The ice in the gully did not move.

At the time of the Iceman's death similar climatic conditions to today probably prevailed. The gully in the rock would have been more or less free of snow and ice. Almost immediately after his death, however, the man along with all his equipment must have been covered by a layer of snow. Before his discovery in 1991, this protective cover appears to have receded and the ice to have melted.

The melting of the glaciers

The only slightly sloping terrain surrounding the location of the find was once covered by a small glacier which flowed eastwards in the direction of the Niederjochferner. When the frontiers were defined in 1922 this area, which is free of ice today, was covered with a 20 m deep layer of packed snow. Due to the warm summers, the melting process had speeded up over the last few years and had reached an unprecedented level by 1991. That winter had been exceptionally warm and had seen very little snow although there had been another cold spell in spring and early summer. The high temperatures in July, August and September led to the rapid melting of the glacier. This was accelerated by a heavy precipitation of Saharan dust which tinged the snow and ice fields yellowish-brown.

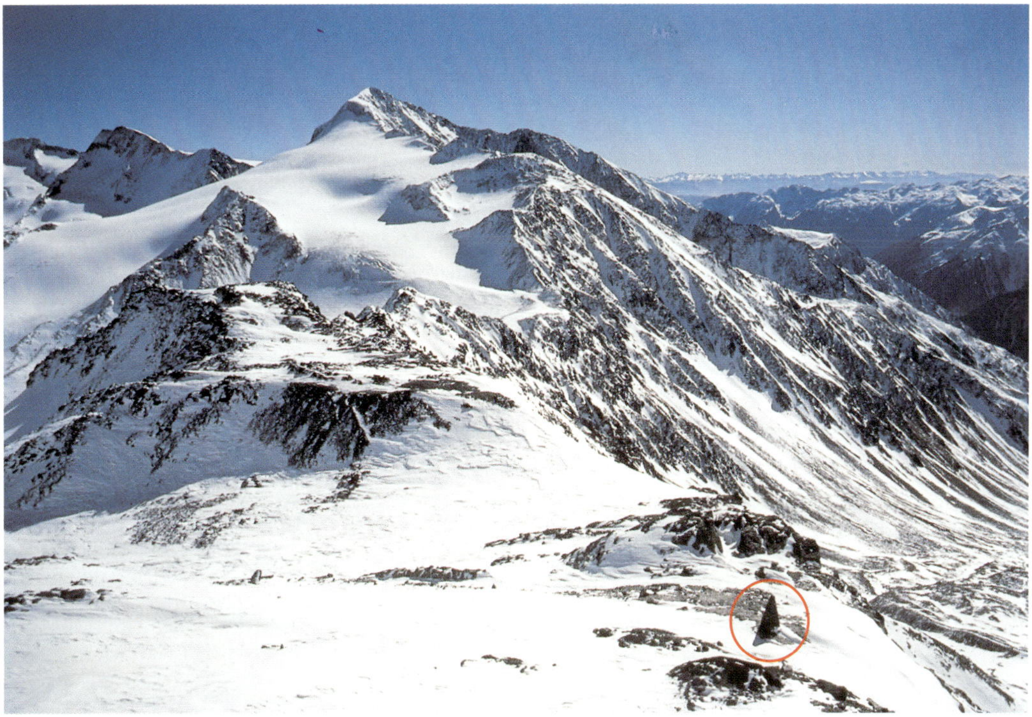

The location of the find near the Tisenjoch

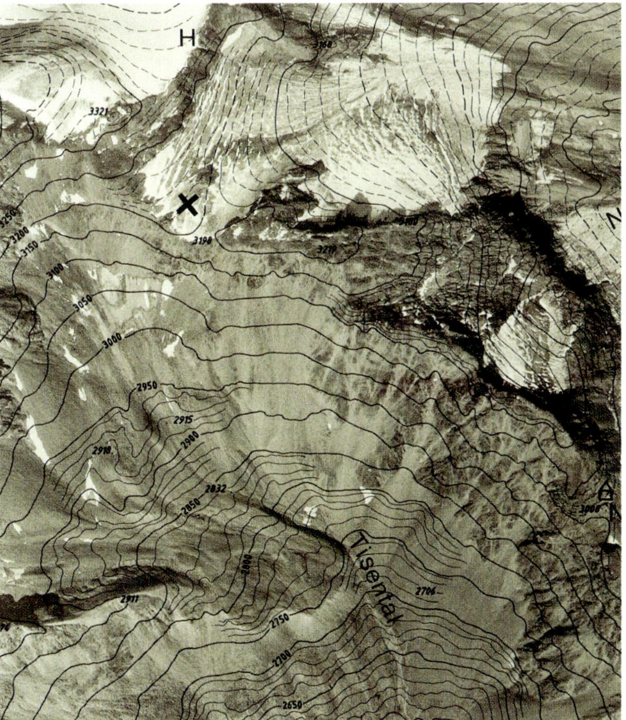

AP Bolzano, photographic map of the province of Bolzano, sheet 1203 Similaun. Photograph taken on 28.09.1985. Authorised for release on the basis of d.I.G.M. N° 88 of 12.02.1988

The recovery

On the day following the find, an Austrian rescue team pressed ahead with the uncovering and rescue of the glacier corpse; it was generally assumed that the person had been the victim of a climbing accident in the 20th century. On account of the high altitude of the location of the find (3,120 m altitude), the rescue team had to be flown in with a helicopter. The body had emerged a further 10 cm from the ice since its discovery and the team tried to totally release it with the help of a pneumatic chisel. Because the meltwater continued to drain into the gully they also had to work under water. It was during this underwater work that the corpse was damaged in the area of the left hip. It was only with great difficulty that the stream of water could be diverted and then after about half an hour the chisel ran out of electricity although the corpse had only been half-freed. Since the weather was getting worse and they did not have the appropriate tools with them, the team was obliged to suspend the work. In order to prove that the body belonged to someone who had been dead at least a hundred years and not to a certain Carlo Capsoni, a music teacher who had gone missing in this area in about 1941, they took an axe blade and its attached haft, which had been lying on a nearby ledge, back with them. Rumours had begun to spread saying that the body had brandmarks on its back and head wounds. They went so far as to maintain that it had been tied up. This led to the initiation of criminal proceedings involving the examination of the body to clarify its identity and to establish whether it had been a victim of crime.

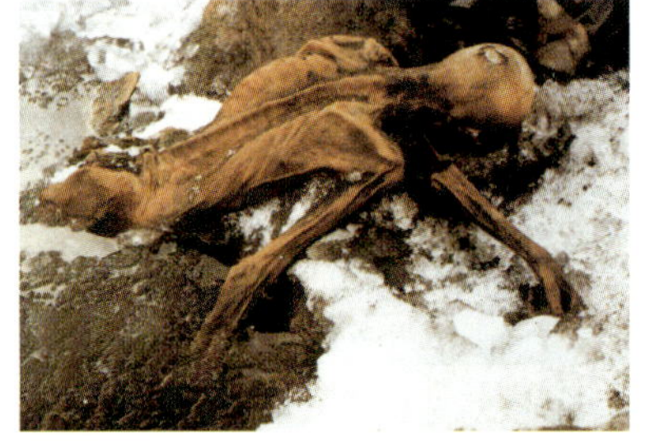
The mummy after the first recovery attempt

On Saturday 21st September 1991 two rock-climbers, Hans Kammerlander and Reinhold Messner, found their way to the location of the find whilst on a South Tyrolean climbing tour. They uncovered the corpse again and lifted the head for the first time. In doing this, parts of the clothing became visible. When they looked for further objects, they found the remains of birch-bark containers, a bow and, as was later established, part of a quiver strut. On Monday 23rd September 1991 an Austrian television crew (ORF) arrived

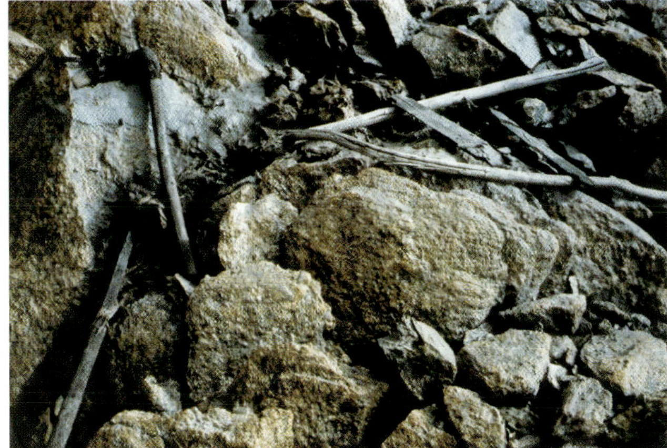

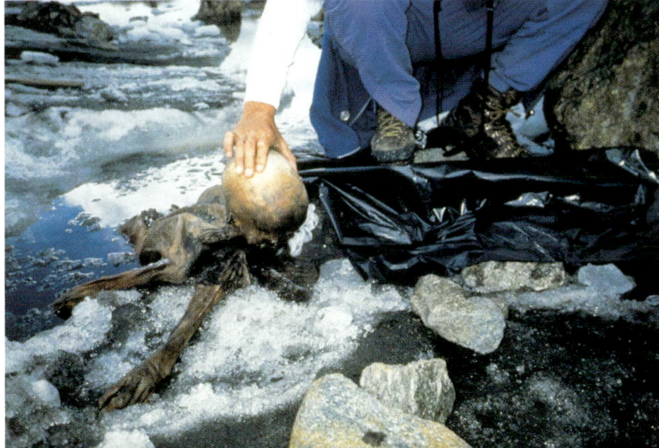

Parts of the Iceman's equipment during the first recovery attempt

The mummy's head is lifted for the first time

at the Tisenjoch. The official recovery of the body took place on the same day in the presence of Prof. Henn from the Institute of Forensic Medicine of the University of Innsbruck. On account of the low temperatures during the night, the body was again frozen stuck. It was finally freed with the help of ice-picks and ski-poles. Bits of leather and fur, string, straps and clumps of hay appeared in the process. These were collected in a pile next to the body. A flint dagger with a wooden haft was also rescued from the meltwater. The recovery was filmed by the camera crew and is therefore very well documented. The glacier mummy was packed into a body bag and sent to Vent in a helicopter and from there to Innsbruck in a hearse along with all the objects found (including the axe which had been kept in

The medicolegal expert, Prof. Rainer Henn (right) on arrival at the location of the find

The body being freed from the ice with the help of ice-axes

Reinhold Messner and Hans Kammerlander visiting the site on 21.09.1991

The glacier mummy before being taken away by helicopter

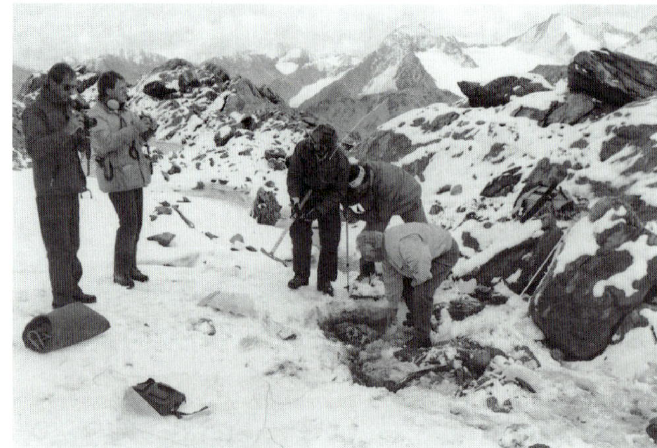

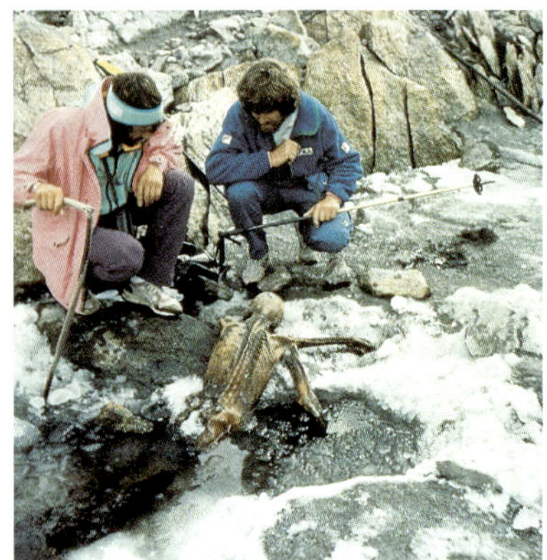

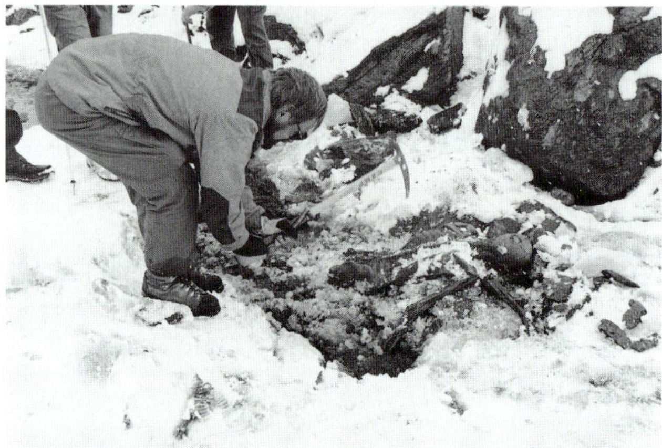

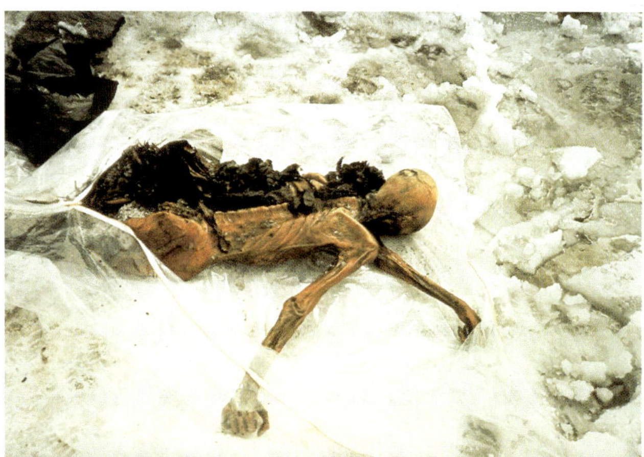

the constabulary in Sölden). Initially, everything was laid out on two operating tables in the Institute of Forensic Medicine.

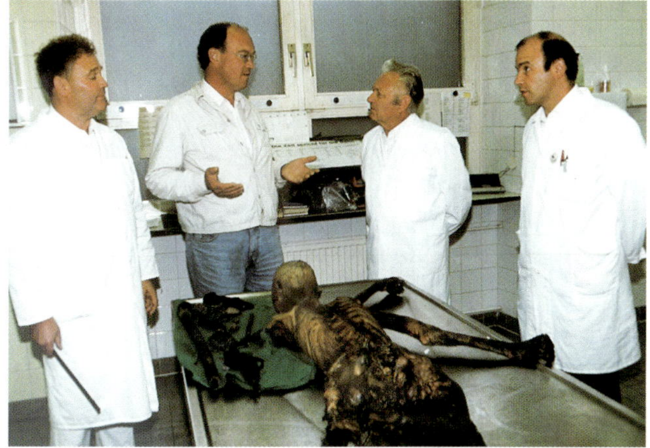

The first archaeological examination of the Tisenjoch find on 24.09.91 in the dissecting room of the Institute of Forensic Medicine at Innsbruck University

In the forensic dissecting room

On the following Tuesday morning, Prof. Dr. Konrad Spindler from the Institute for Primeval and Early History was notified. On the basis of the axe he estimated the entire find to date back to the Bronze Age. A series of photographs went round the world which created an absolute sensation. The Institute in Innsbruck was subjected to an onslaught from the media. In the meantime, the mummy had thawed out to the temperature of 18 °C. On the same evening it was trans-

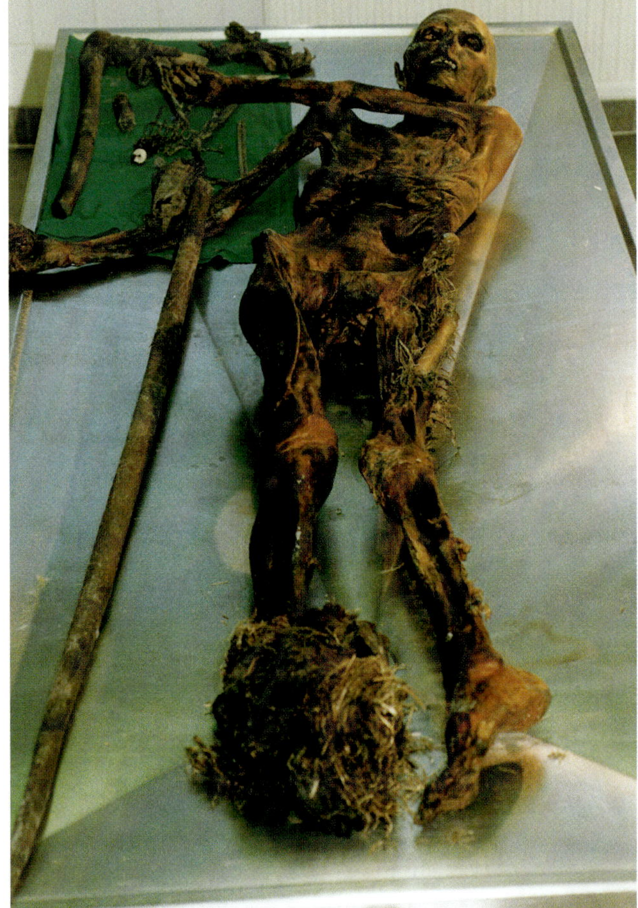

The Iceman and the other finds on the dissecting table

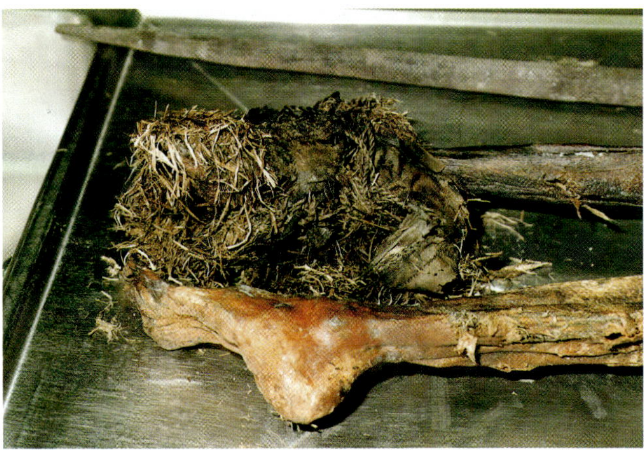

The right shoe was still on the dead man's foot when he was found

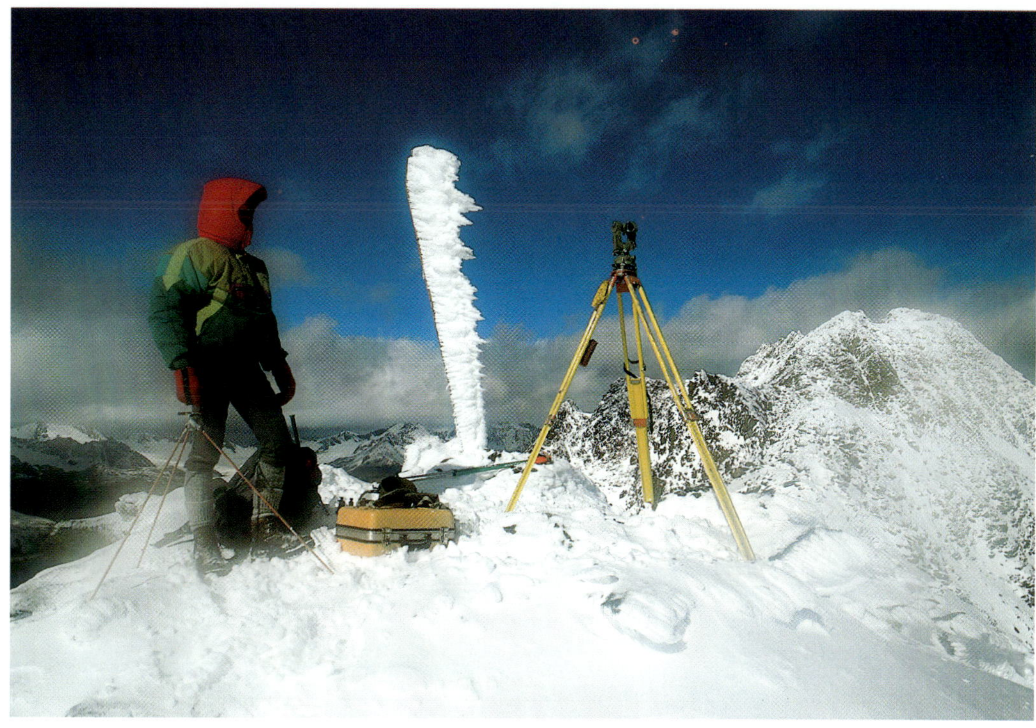

Surveying the site

ferred to the Institute of Anatomy and stored in a refrigeration chamber at – 6 °C and with a humidity of 98 %, thus artificially simulating the conditions on the glacier. The corpse had been previously dabbed with a diluted carbolic solution. In the meantime, the Römisch-Germanischen Zentralmuseum in Mainz had been contacted and had agreed to assume the responsibility for the correct storage and the conservation of the entire find immediately.

Melting the ice with steam drills

Excavation work at the site. The sheet of ice was between 60 and 100 cm thick and covered with a fresh layer of snow at the time of the excavation

The almost ice-free rocky gully

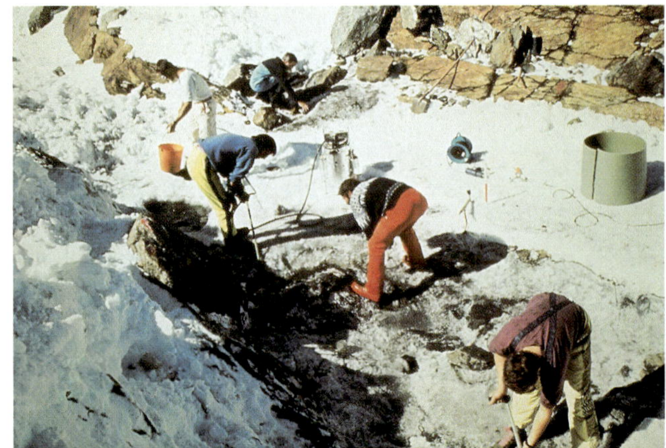

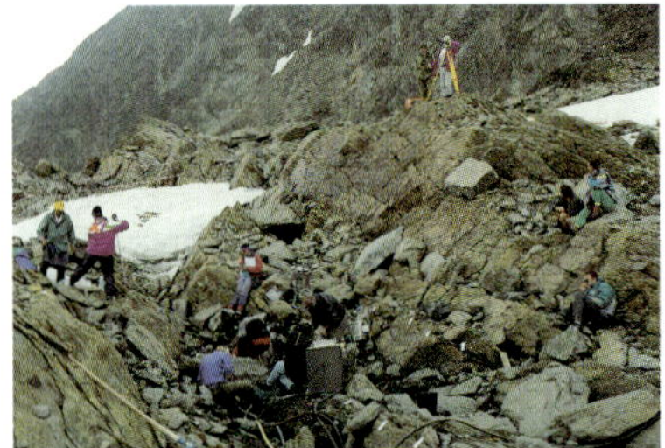

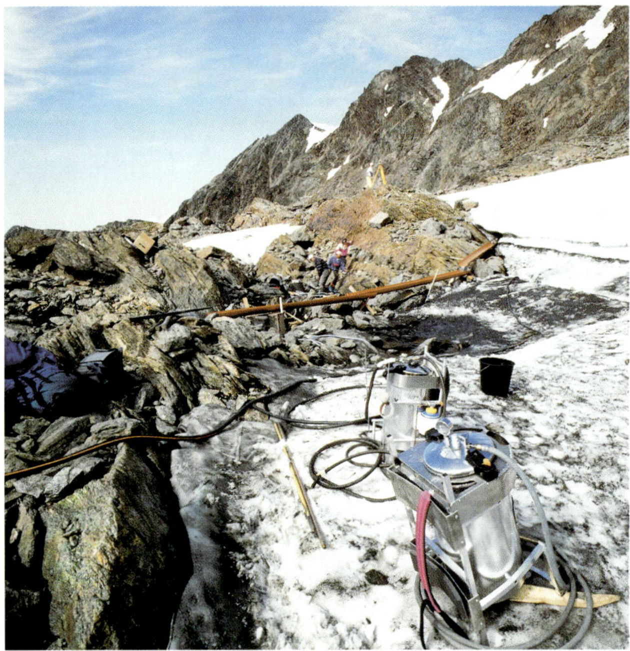

The second survey of the location of the find

In the meantime, repeated speculation that the body had in fact been found on Italian territory made the clarification of the border question necessary. The confusion was caused by the fact that in the Treaty of St.-Germain-en-Laye between the Republic of Austria and the Allied and Associated Forces in 1919 the border was drawn along the watershed between the Inn and the Adige valleys. The corpse was found in an area which now drains off towards the Inn. At the time of defining the borders, however, it was not clear on which side the area of the Tisenjoch was because it was covered by the glacier. In spite of the topographic changes, the borders laid down after the First World War are still valid according to international law. On account of the important find, an official new survey of the border region was necessary. It was established that the location of the find was on South Tyrolean territory 92.56 m from the frontier. As a result, the Province of South Tyrol claimed property rights. The find was, however, entrusted to the University of Innsbruck for scientific examination.

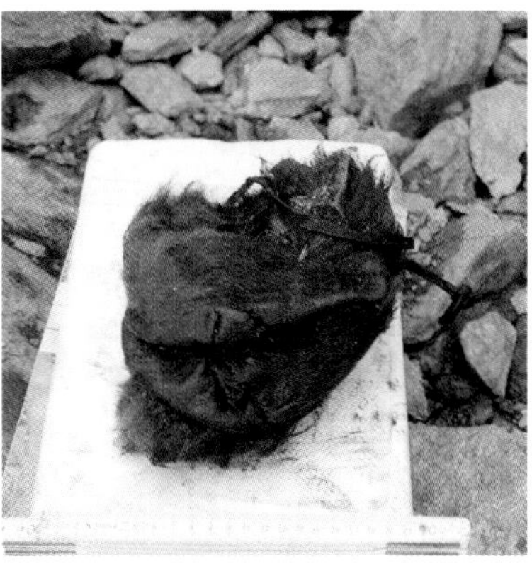

The bearskin cap after the discovery

The examinations of the site

A first examination of the location of the find was carried out between 3rd and 5th October 1991. First the place where the body had been found and the ledge of rock where the objects had been deposited were re-examined. A detailed recording and survey of the whole area and its contour lines followed. The fresh snow which had fallen in the previous few days had to be removed before the work could begin. A steam-blower and dryer were used for the excavation. Near to where the mummy was found, bits of a net made out of grass rope and the remains of a birch-bark container with its contents still in it were found, as well as diverse pieces of fur and leather. On the small stone slab on which the mummy had lain, the remains of a grass cloak were discovered. The oncoming snowy winter prevented further archaeological examinations. A further examination of the site was planned for the following year, 1992. The responsibility for carrying out the work was in the hands of the South Tyrol Ancient Monuments Office in Bolzano, represented by Dr. Lorenzo Dal Ri and Dr. Hans Nothdurfter. The University of Trento commissioned Prof. Bernardino Bagolini and the University of Innsbruck Prof. Dr. Andreas Lippert for the work. The second examination of the site was scheduled from 20th July to 25th August. The first task was shovelling away huge amounts of snow. The meltwater from a higher snowfield kept filling the gully and had to be diverted. Even the base water had to be diverted and repeatedly sieved. A whole range of small finds were discovered in the sediment in the gully. Alongside the remains of further pieces of equipment such as bits of leather and fur, grass and string etc. were also bits of skin, muscle tissue, hair and a finger nail. Even the end of the bow-stave which had had to be abandoned the year before and still remained stuck in the ice was recovered. Finally, a fur cap was found on the stone slab on which the body had lain.

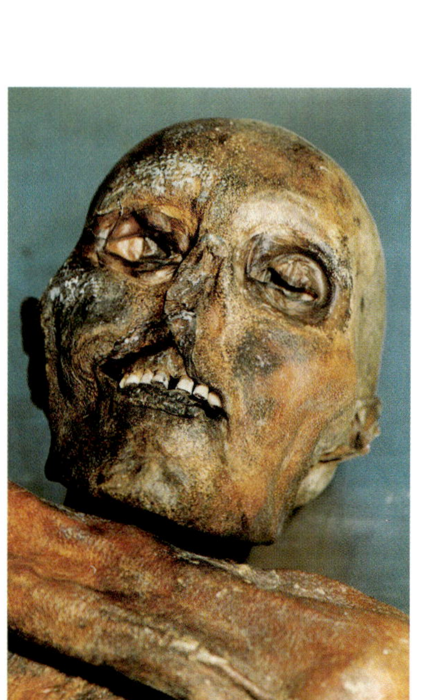

The man's face bears traces of the pressure of the ice

The mummy

For the very first time in the history of medicine and of archaeology anatomical studies can be carried out on a corpse clearly dating back to the 4th millennium B. C. With the exception of damage to the left hip area, the body is practically intact. Because of its position on the rock the face is slightly squashed. The results of the anthropological examination correspond to bone material from the Neolithic Period from the Circum-Alpine area. An examination of the gender of the mummy, which could not be definitively established when it was first discovered, was carried out in the Anatomical Institute and revealed it to be male. The equipment also pointed clearly in this direction. The man was 1.59 m tall.

All the mummy's hair had fallen out in the process of mummification but human hair was found amongst the numerous wisps of hair found on the clothes. The preserved hair is at the most 9 cm long and was dark brown to black in colour. The man most probably wore a beard. Closer examination of the hair revealed that the man must have come into contact with copper ore processing. The finger and toenails had also fallen out. One single fingernail was recovered in the first examination of the site.

Medical examinations

With the help of modern visual techniques, anatomical peculiarities and mutations due to illness could be identified on the body including a missing tooth in the upper jaw and the lack of any sign of wisdom teeth. Particularly noticeable is the extent to which the teeth are worn down through chewing. The main reason for this could be the eating of grain contaminated with the quartz dust of the stone mills on which it was ground. The teeth were otherwise completely free from caries. The front left-hand side of the upper jaw showed pronounced wear, suggesting some unknown regular daily activity.

In addition, the Iceman has no twelfth pair of ribs. This rare anomaly had no negative consequences for him. The man has a well-healed serial break of the ribs on the left-hand side of the chest. However, unhealed fractured ribs could also be identified on the right-hand side of the chest. The reason for this could either be an accident shortly before his death or the pressure of the ice. The same is true of a break in his left upper arm. A cyst-like mutation on the little toe of his left foot could have been due to frostbite. The examination of the one fingernail revealed that the Iceman had suffered high degrees of stress months before he died. Alongside degenerative changes he also showed quite pronounced vascular sclerosis. Pictures of approximately 700 transaxial sections of the

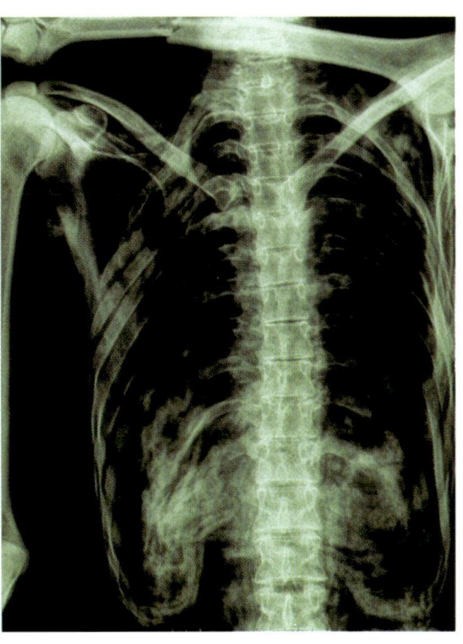

Radiological examination of the thorax. A deformity of the left side of the ribcage is visible

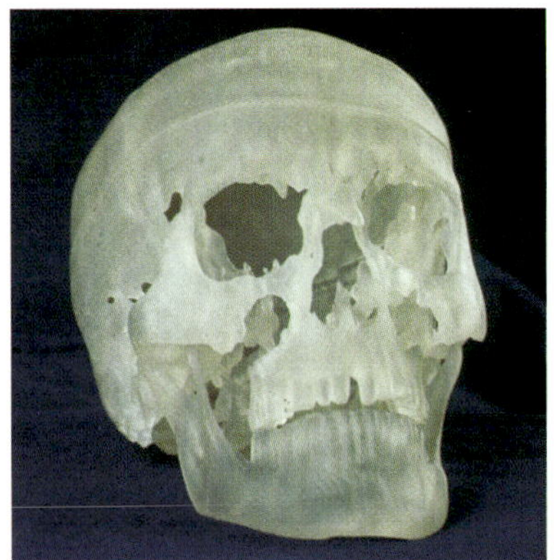

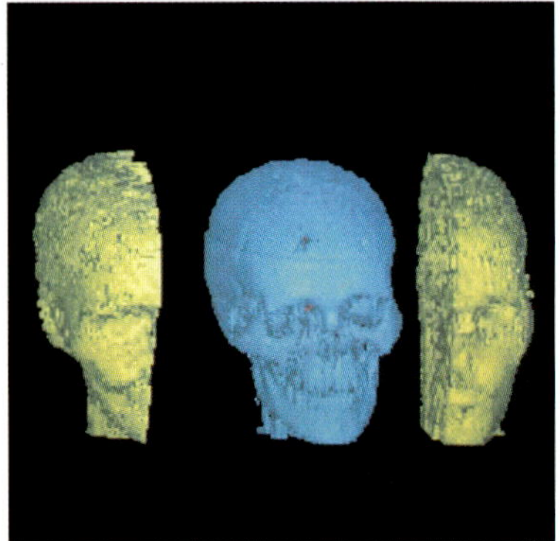

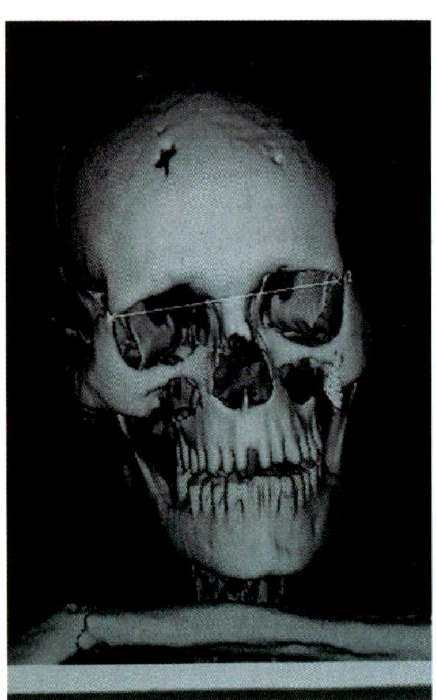

mummy were taken using computer tomography. On these, one can see the internal organs, some of which are totally shrunken and out of place due to the position of the body. This data also formed the basis for the three-dimensional representation of the skeleton construction which was made using stereolithography. It was, for example, possible to create a model of the skull within 40 hours which was accurate to a fraction of a millimetre. Some parts of the skull show deformities due to the position in which it lay. The technique of stereolithography which was first developed on the Iceman has since been successfully applied in medical practice.

The greatest challenge of the medical research programme was, without doubt, the endoscopic examination of the mummy. Special high-precision instruments had to be made specially out of titanium for the tricky micro-surgical interventions. In order to get samples of the internal organs a window was cut into the skin and pincers introduced along with a special highly sensitive optical lens. This made it possible to inspect and visually document e.g. the larynx, the heart and lung area, the liver, the main arteries, the digestive system and the brain. Slight arterial calcification could be established at the base of the brain. The samples of tissue which were taken are being further examined. The contents of the stomach and large intestine have already been established. Further revelations concerning the living conditions and the state of health of the man are expected once the endoscopic examination of the mummy has been completed. DNA analysis revealed that the man was of Alpine origin. Between the discovery of the mummy and its transportation from Innsbruck to Bolzano no fewer than 570 inspections were carried out on the body and 100 samples taken. The largest samples weighed 60 milligrams; altogether the samples weighed a little over a gramme.

The age

In order to establish the age of the mummy a small cylinder of bone was taken from the left thigh. With the help of samples of thin slices of bone, the components of the bone cortex (osteone), which change with age, could be established and counted at the Osteological Research Laboratory of the University of Stockholm and at the Institute of Anatomy of the University of Innsbruck. The age-related signs of wear and the changes in the bone structure visible in the X-ray pictures also had to be taken into account. On the basis of the analyses, a minimum age of 40 and a maximum age of 53 were determined. The average of various calculations gives an age of 46. The Iceman thus reached an advanced age by Neolithic standards.

Stereolithographic model of the skull

Three-dimensional representation of the soft and bony parts of the skull

3D reconstruction of the skull after a spiral computer tomogramme

The tattoos

Already at the time of discovery, marks were found on the mummy's back which were first thought to be brandings. It was later established that these were tattoos. On account of the bluish colour it can be assumed that they were done with charcoal. The tattoos consist of a series of streaks and crosses. A total of four series of streaks can be found on the left of the lumbar vertebra and one on the right. Three further series of streaks are tattooed onto the left calf and more on the arch of the right foot and on the inner and outer ankle joint. Both the inner side of the right knee and the left-hand side of the left Achilles tendon bear a cruciform mark. Two weals on the left wrist joint were, however, caused by a tightly drawn strap. This indicates that the man held something in his hand. In prehistoric times, tattoos were done for various reasons. It is thought, however, that they were mainly used for medicinal purposes. In the case of the Iceman, it was noticeable that the tattoos were concentrated mainly in the lumber region, on the knees and on the ankle joints – i. e. areas which are subject to most strain. These areas actually

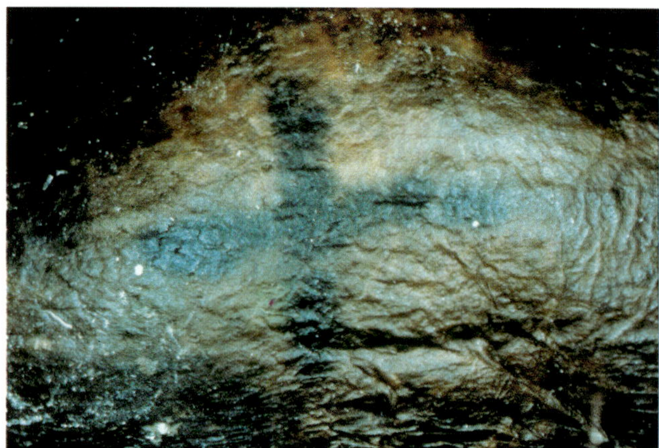

The cruciform tattoo on the inside of the right knee

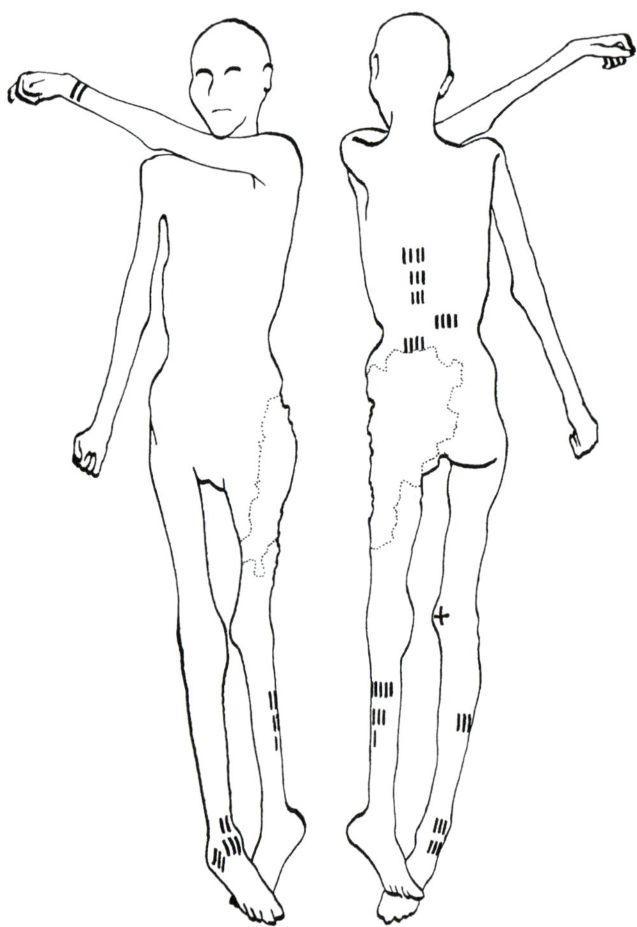

View of all the tattoos found on the mummy's body

did show signs of age and stress-related erosion, whereby a link could be established between the tattoos and the radiological findings on the neighbouring bones. More than once the Iceman had undergone pain-relieving treatment as can be observed in the most diverse cultures.

The mummification process

In the course of mummification, the corpse was subject to a dehydration process which gives the skin its tough leathery appearance today. The skin colour varies considerably, ranging from very light beige-brown to brown-black. The mummy was not totally dried out through the dehydration process but could still be moved following its recovery. It now weights 13.03 kg; the original body weight must have been around 50 kg. The physical position of the man's body probably corresponds to the one it was in when he died although the pressure of the ice could also have altered its position.

The man had reached the then ice-free gully in the rock which had evidently been used by other human-beings long before him. He had carefully deposited his equipment on the surrounding rocks. The reasons or conditions of his death can no longer be proven but he most likely died of exposure. How the mummification proceeded is not yet clear but it is thought that the body and the other findings were covered with a protective layer of snow. Snow stays permeable to air for years and mummification happens through freeze-drying. Only after years does the snow turn to ice and thus brings the whole process to a close. The location of the find must have been covered by an approximately 20 m thick mass of ice. Since it lay in a protected gully, the main glacier flowed straight over it; however, the sheer weight and the reverberations which could well have reached the very bottom of the gully did lead to small changes in position. It is, for example, thought that the Iceman originally lay on his left side and was turned onto his front in the course of time.

There is another theory which posits that the mummification process took place without a protective covering of snow, on the surface so to speak, and that the snow or ice came later. This is contradicted by the fact that the corpse would have been exposed to insects and, even more so, to wild animals. In addition, the location is unprotected from the winds and the original position of the laid off gear, particularly the light birch-bark container, would not have been maintained. The findings were positioned on a somewhat higher ledge in the rock and emerged sooner from the melting ice than the corpse itself, a fact which is corroborated by their state of decay.

The preservation

The essential precondition for further research to take place is the preservation of the mummy. This is why the natural preservation must be replaced by an artificial one by recreating the natural conditions on the glacier as closely as possible with technical aids. At the Institute of Anatomy of the University of Innsbruck the mummy was conserved in a refrigeration chamber at a temperature of – 6 °C. In order to achieve maximum air humidity, the mummy was wrapped in a sterile operation sheet and surrounded by crushed ice. A plastic tarpaulin was laid on top. This, in turn, was covered with more ice and then wrapped up in yet another plastic sheet. In this manner, an air humidity of 98 %, i.e. more or less that of the glacier which has 100 %, was obtained.

The dating

Following the unique discovery, the findings were subjected to radiocarbon or carbon-14 dating. In order to do this, bone particles and fibrous tissue were taken from the left hip. The samples were examined by the Research Laboratory for Archaeology and History of Art in Oxford and by the Institut für Mittelenergiephysik of the Federal Technical College in Zurich. Botanical material was also subjected to examination. Fragments of the grass stalks of the cloak were used for this purpose. The vegetable material was sent to the Svedberg Laboratoriet of the University of Uppsala and to the Centre des Faibles Radioactives in Paris. The data from the samples examined in the various laboratories all led to very similar results: the Iceman lived between 3350 and 3100 B. C.

The clothing

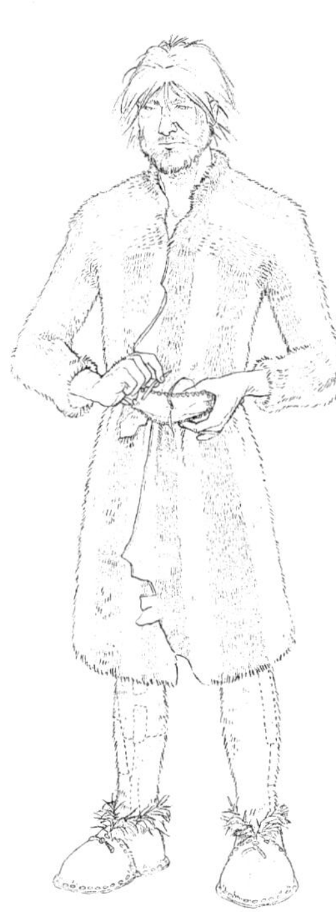

Reconstruction of the Iceman with his clothes and equipment

The upper garment

A few fragments of the Iceman's upper garment have survived. These have been pieced together in the restoration workshop of the Römisch-Germanischen Zentralmuseum in Mainz. They mainly consist of pieces of hide from a domestic goat which would have been worn with the hair on the outside, although most of the hair has fallen out. On the inside, there are traces of scraping which would have come from the cleaning of the hide. Examinations suggest that the hide was tanned using grease and smoke. The garment consisted of numerous long, rectangular strips of skin which were joined together by regular oversewing on the inside. The arrangement of the skin in vertical strips may have been with the intent of making a pattern out of the different colours; the darker strips alternated with the lighter ones. Animal sinews were used as thread. The dirt on the inside and the repairs with grass thread indicate that this piece of clothing had been in use for some time. A reconstruction concludes that the garment was worn open in front. Since there are no signs of a fastening it can be assumed that the garment was closed with a belt. Whilst few horizontally sewn pieces of skin from the shoulders of the garment have been preserved, there are no remains of sleeves. It is open to speculation whether it ever actually had sleeves. The whole garment probably reached down to the knees.

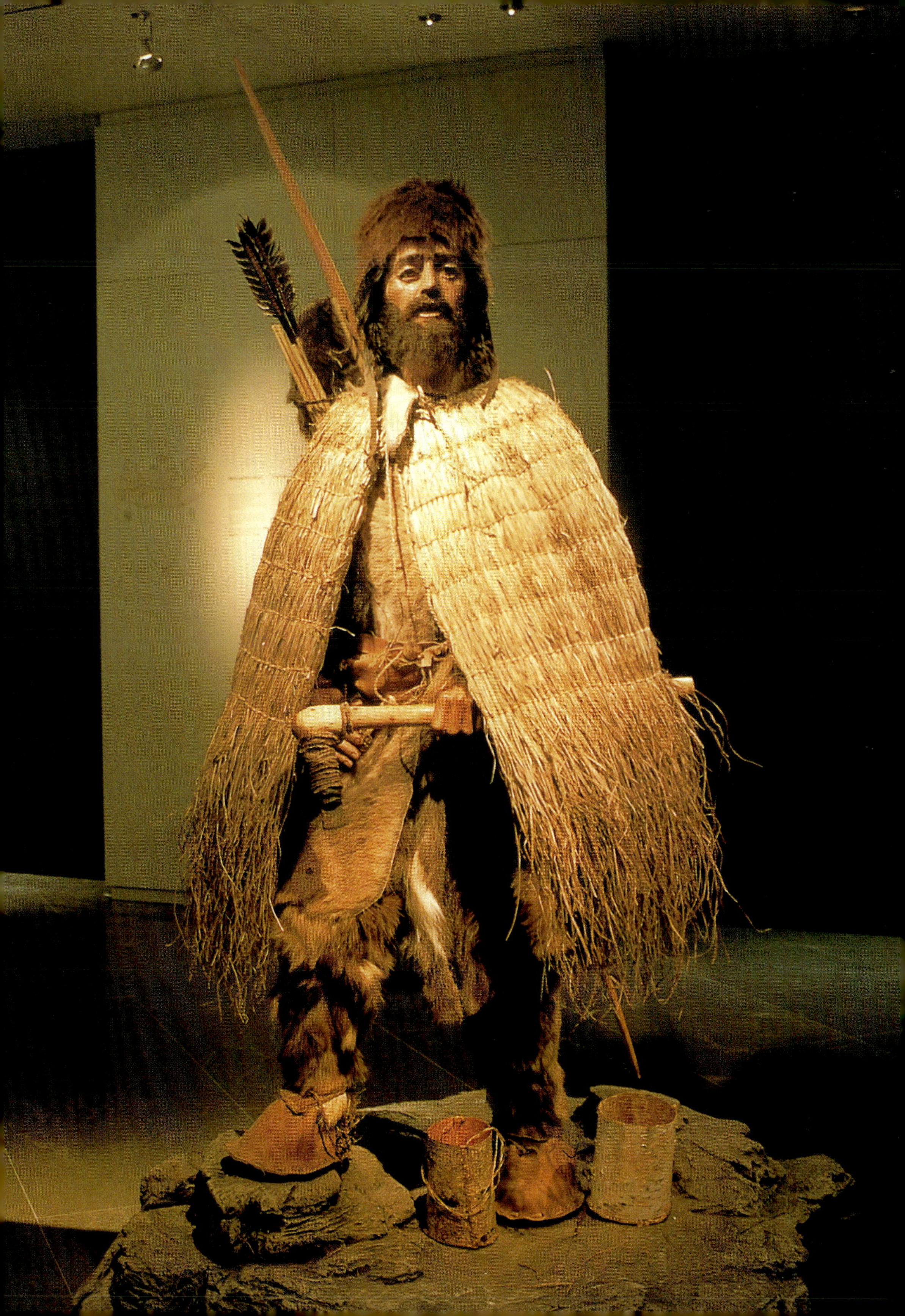

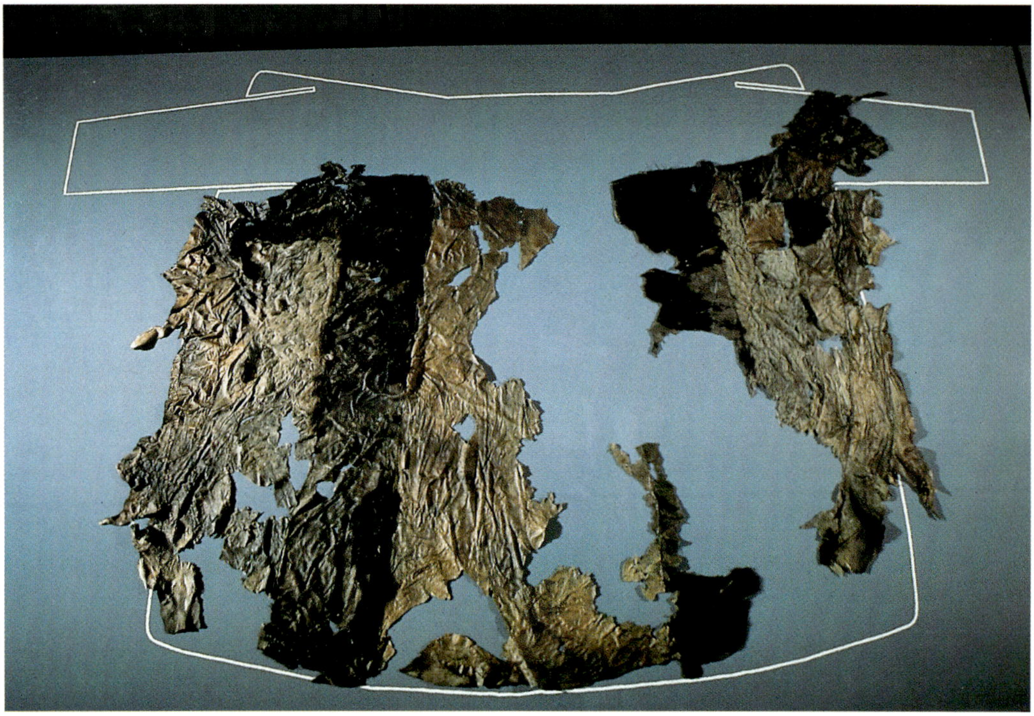

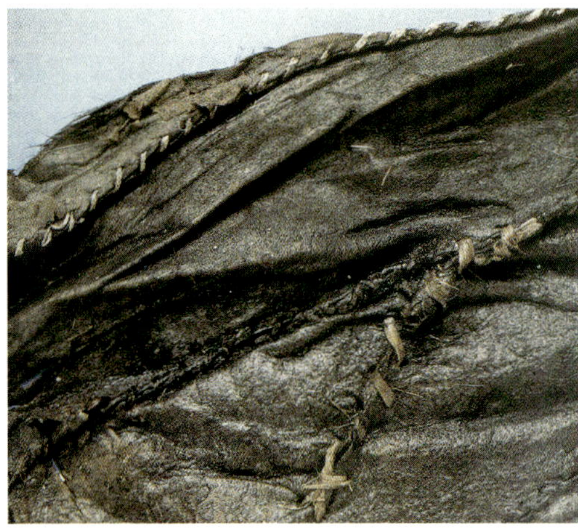

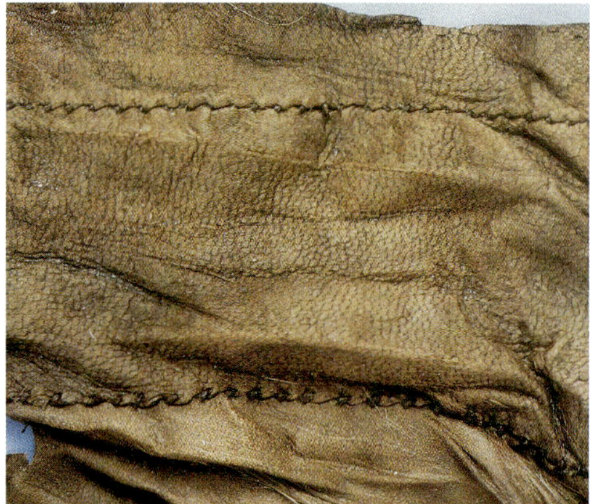

The upper garment is made of strips of domestic goat hide

The garment was mended with rough stitches

The mostly longitudinal strips of hide were neatly sewn together with regular stitches

The leggings

Observations from the location of the find testify that the Iceman had a covering on each leg. These were composed of a number of pieces of skin sewn together which are more recent the further down they go. They are made of the hide of a domestic goat. The leg protection was approximately 65 cm long and covered the thighs and lower legs. It was, therefore, not really a pair of trousers. The bow-shaped top was reinforced with a leather strip which was threaded through and knotted onto the belt using the two laces which were attached to it. There was a deerskin strap sewn onto the other end of the leg protection which could be tied down when doing up the shoes. This prevented it from riding up. The leg protection had evidently had a lot of use and had often been repaired. This type of leg protection, so-called "leggings", was used by the North American Indians well into the 19th century.

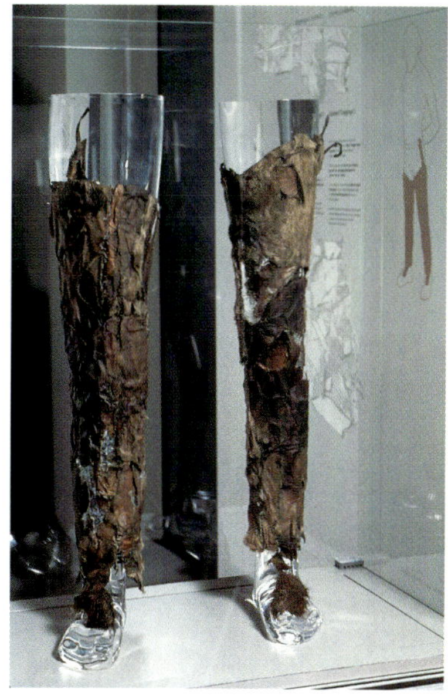

The leggings were made of pieces of domestic goat hide and knotted onto the belt with thongs

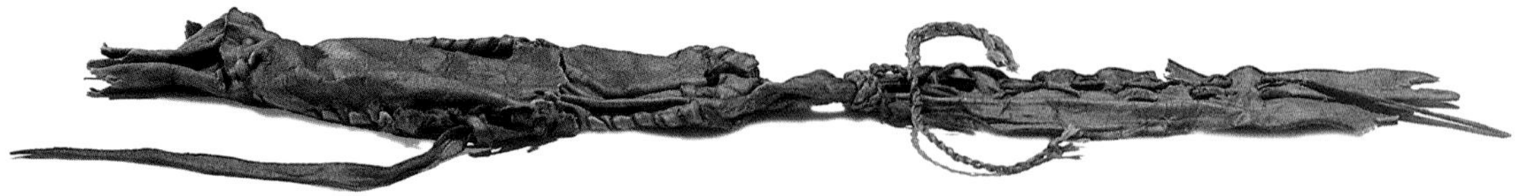

The belt

The Iceman's gear also included a, not entirely preserved, belt. It was made of a 4–4.8 cm wide calf-leather strap. A piece of sewn-on leather formed a pouch. The longitudinal sides of the opening were strengthened with decorative stitches. The opening could be closed with a narrow leather thong. The fragments show that the belt originally was almost 2 m long and therefore reached around the hips twice.

The little pouch contained five items, including a scraper, a drill and a flint flake. A 7.1 cm bone awl was also found. A black mass which could be identified as "true tinder" fungus filled most of the bag. This was used to kindle fire and therefore constituted a sort of prehistoric fire-lighter which had, above all, to be kept dry. Fine traces of pyrites show that lumps of pyrites were used to create sparks. None were found in the equipment of the Iceman however.

The leather pouch attached to the belt was worn around the waist

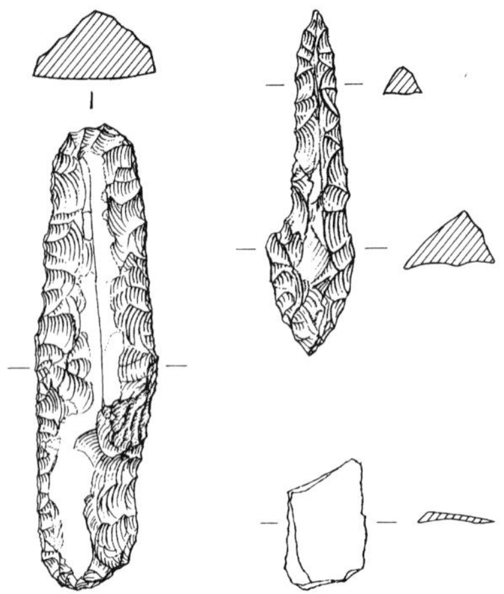

The contents of the leather pouch: flint blade, flint drill, small flint blade and bone awls

The loincloth

Amongst the surviving bits of hide was a 50 cm long and 33 cm wide leather fragment. This piece of clothing consisted of long narrow strips of goat hide joined by oversewing with animal sinews. It is thought that the originally approximately 1 m long apron would have been drawn between the legs and fastened at the front and back with the belt. Such loincloths were also worn by North American Indians.

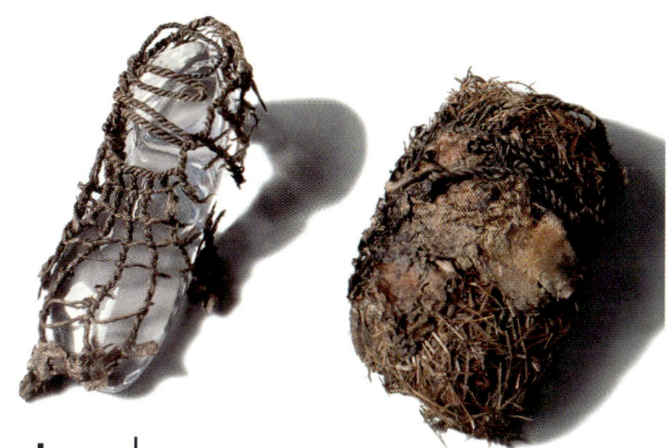

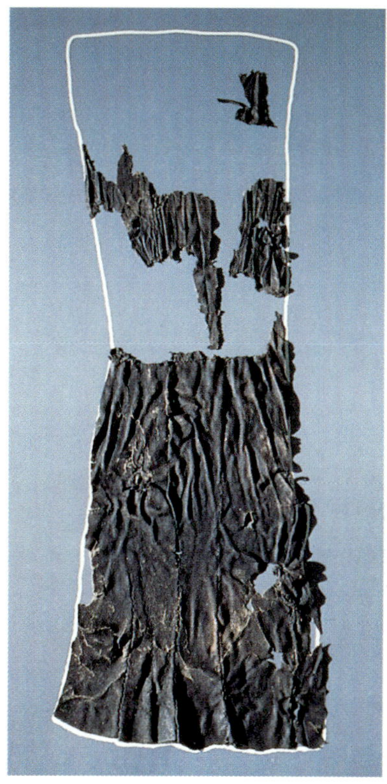

The Iceman's shoes

The goat hide loincloth

Drawing of the right shoe with its grass inlay

The shoes

The Iceman wore shoes on both feet. The right shoe was still on the foot when the mummy was recovered and was taken off for restoration. The left shoe was not so well preserved. The one shoe consists of an oval leather sole with turned up edges held in place with a leather thong. A net woven out of grass was attached to this on the inside to hold in place the hay which was stuffed inside as protection against the cold. The shoe was closed with a leather upper which was attached to the sole with a leather thong. Contrary to the sole leather, the upper leather was worn with the hair facing outwards. The shaft around the ankle was bound with grass filaments to prevent the damp from getting in. There was a strip of leather running diagonally across the sole of the shoe which was supposed to give it some kind of grip. Whereas the sole of the shoe is made of brown bear skin, the uppers are made of deerskin. The uppers were closed using "shoe-laces".

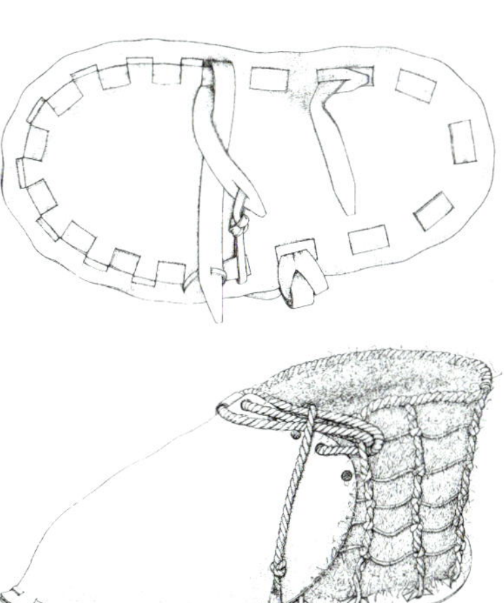

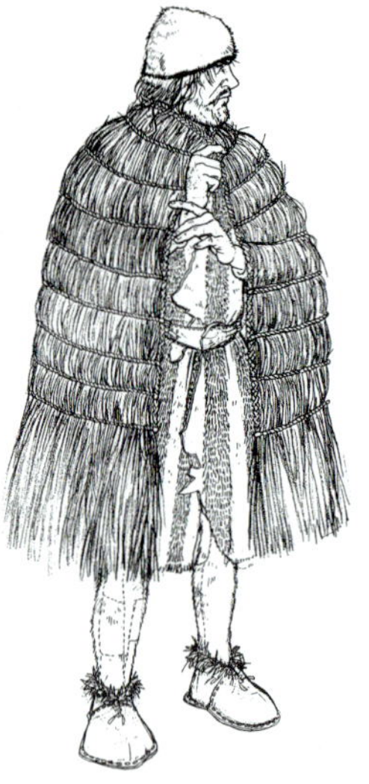

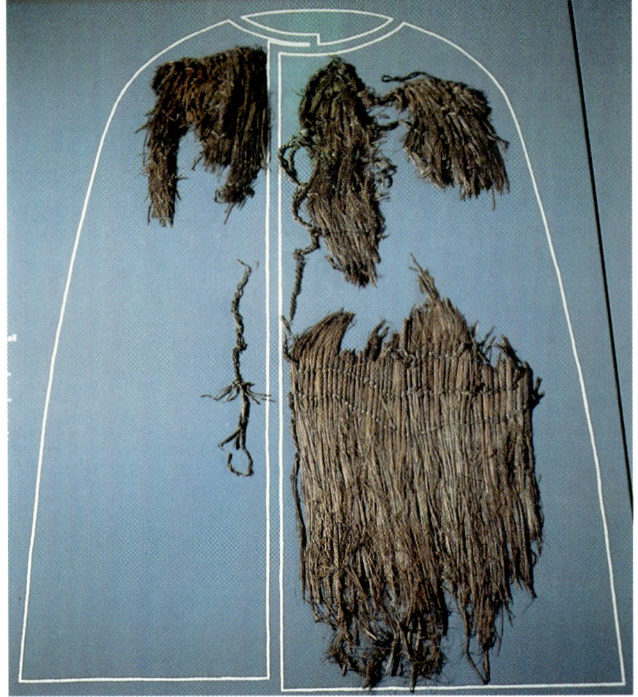

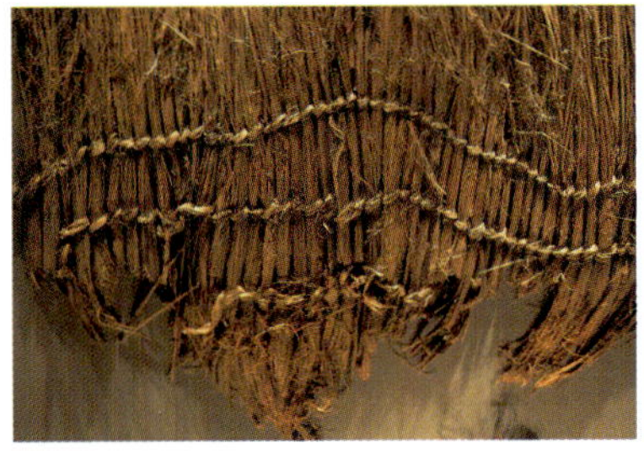

Detail of the grass weave

The Iceman wore a grass cloak to protect himself from the rain

The grass cloak

Three larger pieces of plaited grass were recovered in the follow-up examination of the site where the corpse was found. These were first thought to constitute a mat. However, the examination in Mainz showed that these were parts of a loose, sleeveless cloak. The cloak was worn over the top of the skin clothing. The original length must have been around 90 cm. This would have covered the entire torso and probably also the thighs. The cloak was made of long stalks of an Alpine grass. The neck of the cloak is plaited in a simple twine arrangement around the top. A number of grass cords are attached to this at regular intervals the use of which is not known. The cloak was open at the front. The longitudinal edges are sewn with grass threads. Attached to these are horizontal cords which at regular intervals of 6–7 cm are woven into the cloak. Below this, the vertical grasses hang down freely in a sort of curtain which gave the wearer freedom of movement for his legs. Grass and straw cloaks were worn right into the 20th century, above all by shepherds as effective protection against the rain.

The cap

During the second examination of the site the headgear was found. This was a half-spherical skin cap consisting of a number of strips of skin. The cap was made of the pelt of a brown bear and, as opposed to the other pieces of clothing, even the outer fur has remained intact. Two leather thongs were attached to the lower rim of the cap with the purpose of tying it under the chin.

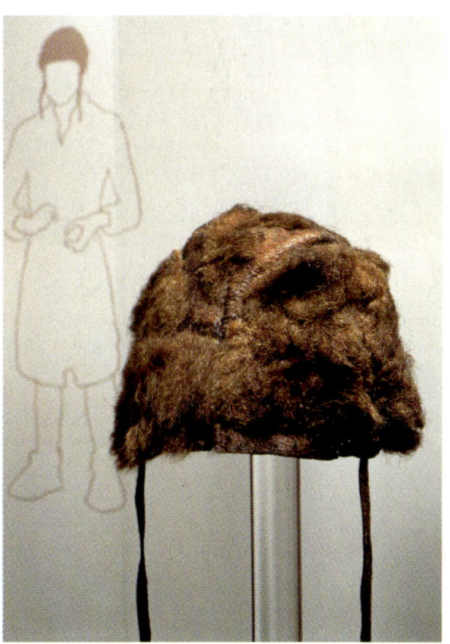

The Iceman's headgear was a bearskin cap

The equipment

The unique aspect of the Tisenjoch find is that a man has been found wearing his everyday clothing and equipped with his usual gear – literally going about his daily business. For the first time we can observe the almost completely preserved clothing of a human-being from the late Neolithic Period. Remains of clothing were so far only discovered in the pile-dwellings in the Circum-Alpine area, whereby these were usually only made of plant fibres. Animal materials such as skins etc. did not survive but nevertheless the usually only fragmentary remains of clothing offer some insight into the contemporary weaving and knotting techniques. On the other hand, the Tisenjoch discovery provides a snapshot of a Copper Age man in a high mountain region. The clothing consists of a cap, an upper garment, leggings, a loincloth, a pair of shoes and a cloak. There were no woven materials used. The threads were made out of animal sinews and occasionally out of plants, mainly out of grasses and to a lesser extent out of bast.

During his stay in the rocky gully, which was free of ice at that time, the Iceman laid down some of his equipment. He put his quiver on a stone slab. He deposited his bow, his axe, a backpack and a birch-bark container on another ledge. The rest he wore on his person. At the time of his

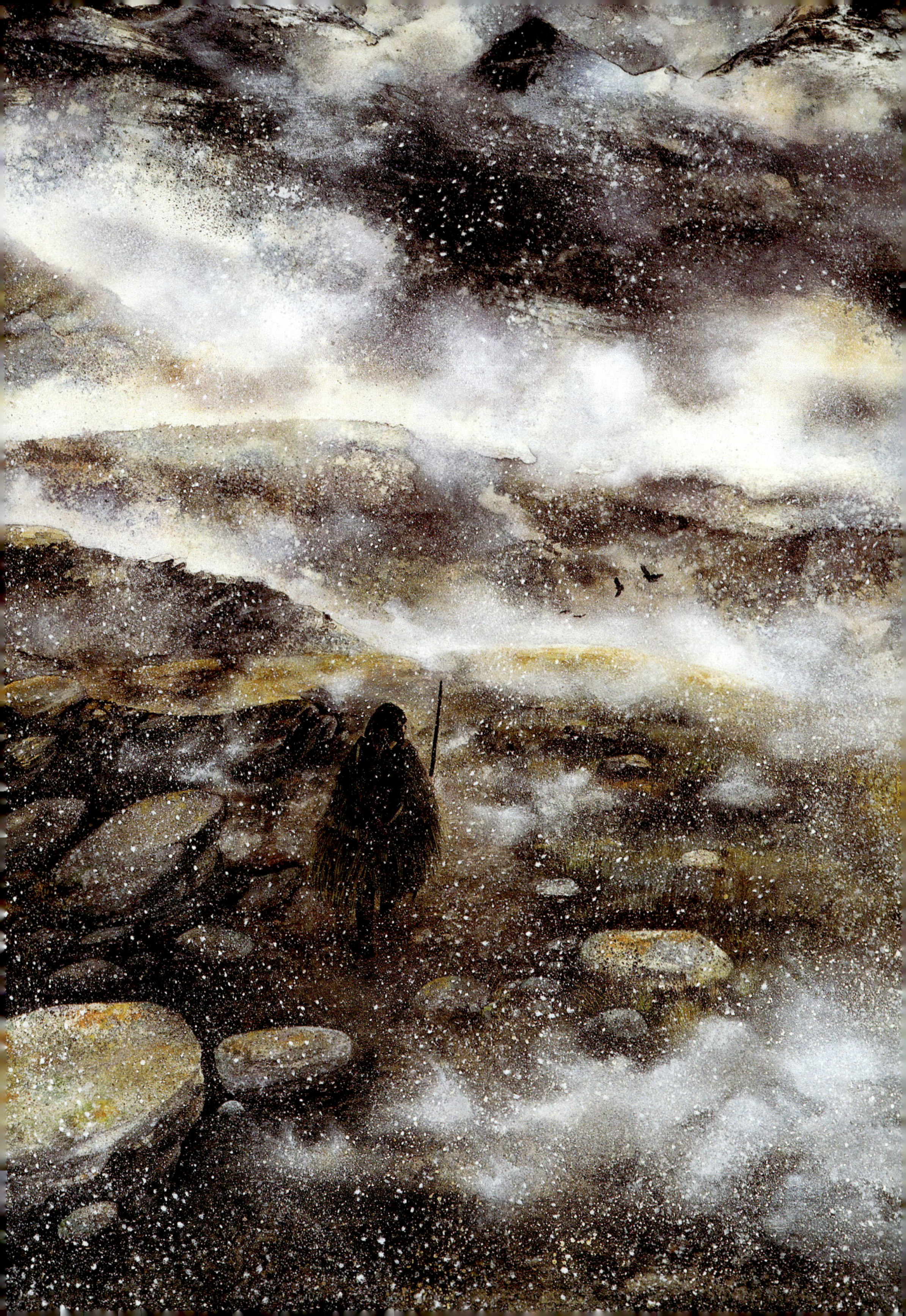

death the man was completely clothed. His cap presumably slipped from his head as he stretched out on the stone slab where he was to be found over 5,000 years later. Whilst the clothing on the front of his body was well-preserved on account of his position, the clothing on his back was probably blown away when the ice receded. This is true above all of the grass cloak.

The axe

Of all the equipment belonging to the Iceman, the first to be found was the axe, which was lying on a ridge away from the corpse along with the bow-stave, diverse bits of string and the backpack. The axe was preserved along with its haft made of yew-wood. At the top of the haft there is a forked shaft with a 6.8 cm deep groove into which the butt of the blade slots. Almost three-quarters of the blade are embedded in the shafting fork and held in place with birch pitch. The top of the shaft was also tightly bound with narrow leather strips which guaranteed a perfect hold. Quite a number of axe shafts have been found in wetland settlements. The Tisenjoch axe is the first totally preserved prehistoric axe. The 9.3 cm long blade is trapeziform in shape. The narrow ends have slightly curved edges. The axe is made of almost pure copper.

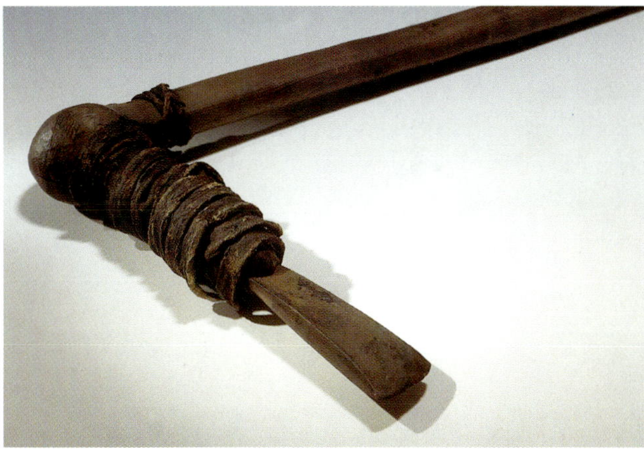

The Tisenjoch axe is the only complete prehistoric axe to have been found to date. It is made up of a haft and a copper blade

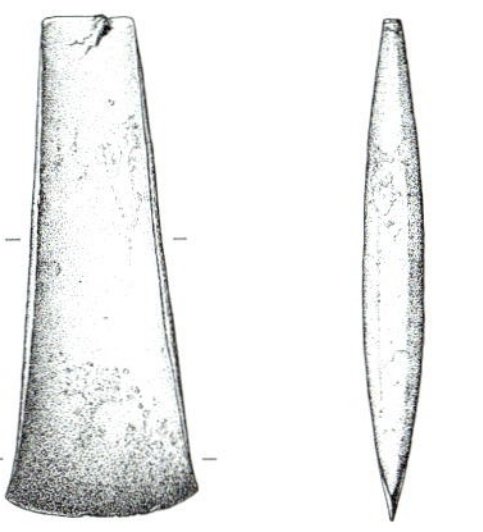

The blade was attached to the haft with tree resin and leather strips

The bow

The largest piece of equipment belonging to the Iceman is a 1.82 m long bow-stave made of yew-wood which is completely preserved. Shortly before his death, the man propped it against the rock. Since the bow-stave was not moved by the ice, it remained in its original position. The bow bears signs of being worked on and is clearly an unfinished, not yet functional piece. The bow-stave is incomplete and the ends lack the necessary chucks to attach the loops of the string.

The quiver and its contents

A completely preserved quiver was discovered on a stone slab approximately 5 m away from the corpse. This was composed of a rectangular, elongated chamois hide bag which was newer towards the bottom. The hair, which was only sparsely preserved, was facing outwards. The piece of hide was held together lengthways and along the lower narrow side by a seam. Along the lengthways seam the quiver is reinforced with a 92.2 cm long hazel rod. This had been stripped of its bark and smoothed and had had a deep V-shaped groove carved into

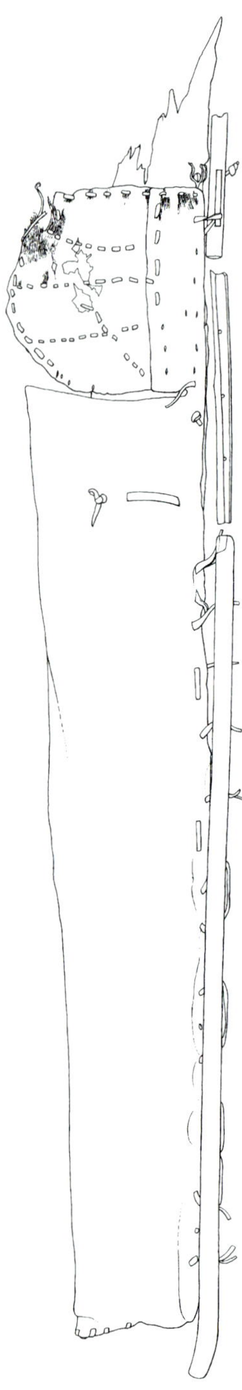

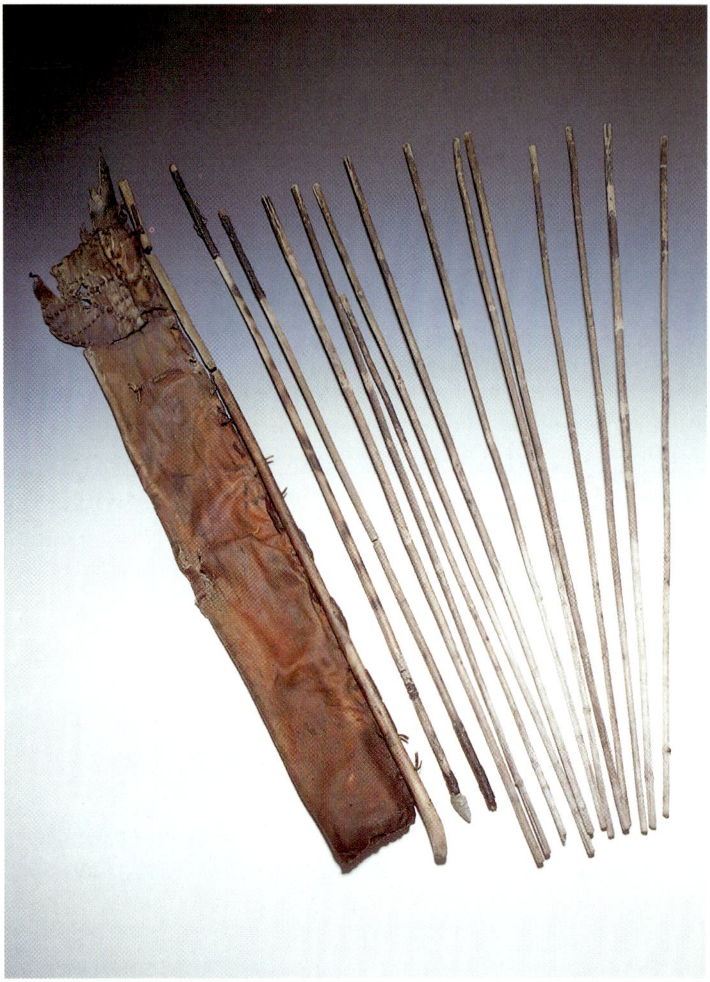

it lengthways. The rod was bored through twenty times at regular intervals along this groove. The lengthways seam of the quiver was finally slotted into this groove and tied on with narrow leather thongs. This reinforcement was broken into three pieces. The man carried the middle fragment on his person. The lid and the strap to carry it with were missing. The quiver contained two arrows ready for shooting and twelve rough shafts. The unfinished shafts are between 84 and 87 cm long and are made of shoots of hard viburnum sapwood. They were stripped of their bark but not yet smoothed down. The wider end of all the shafts is indented. The heads of the finished arrows are made of flint. They had been glued with birch tar and bound on with string. The remains of a three-part radial fletching made of feathers which had been fixed onto the end of the arrow with birch tar and a fine thread were preserved next to them. One arrow had an extra shaft made of cornel wood inserted into the top.

Also in the quiver were the tips of four stag-antlers tied together with strips of bast. They may have been intended for use as arrowheads. A bent antler-point was probably used to skin and gut animals. Finally worth mentioning are some lengths of string made of tree bast wound into a ball and two animal sinews. The string must have been up to 2 m long and could possibly have been the string of a bow.

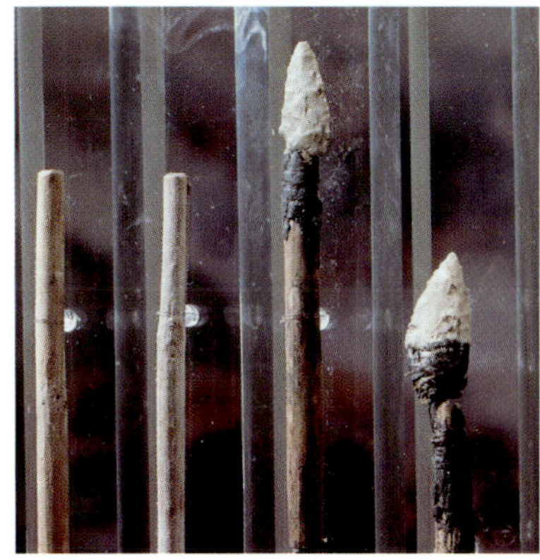

The Iceman's quiver is not totally preserved. The lid and the carrying strap are missing

Two arrows ready to shoot, twelve unfinished shafts, four stag antler tips tied together with a length of bast, a bent antler tip and a cord were found in the quiver

The sharpened flint points were attached to the shafts with tree resin

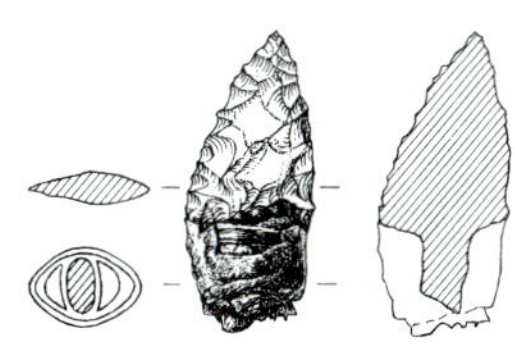

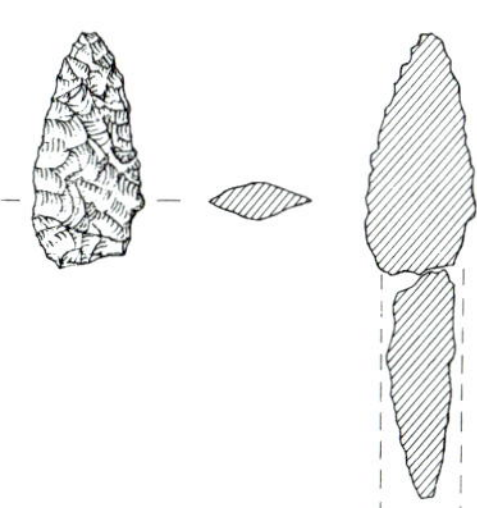

The dagger

An approximately 13.2 cm long flint dagger was discovered very close to the mummy. It has a small triangular flint blade and an ash handle. The tang of the blade had been pushed deep into the slit wooden handle and held in place with sinews. A string was attached to a notch at the end of the handle. The triangular sheath-like scabbard is 12 cm in length and made of knotted limewood bast. To make it a small mat was plaited, folded together and sewn up lengthways with a grass thread. Double plaiting reinforces the opening of the sheath and horizontal wefts in twisted yarn are worked into the sheath at regular intervals. A leather eye on the side presumably allowed the sheath to be attached to the belt.

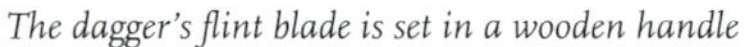

The dagger's flint blade is set in a wooden handle

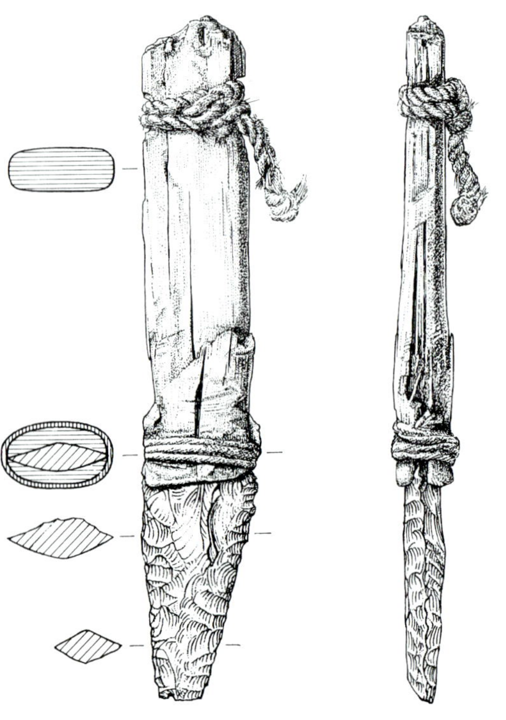

The retoucheur

Among the most unusual objects in the man's equipment is a retoucheur. The implement is made of a section of a stripped lime-tree branch which has been cut off straight at one end and appears to have been sharpened at the other end. A 6.1 cm long rod was stuck into the medullary canal at this end. The tool has a total length of 11.9 cm whereby the spike sticks out no more than 4 mm. This part was also hardened by firing. Analyses show that it was made of stag-antler. The tool was used for the more intricate work in the production of flint implements. When the head of the tool grew blunt through use, it could be sharpened like a pencil and thus rendered fully functional again. The retoucheur is the only known example of its kind. Experimental archaeological tests have shown that it fulfils its function perfectly.

The retoucheur was used to sharpen the stone implements

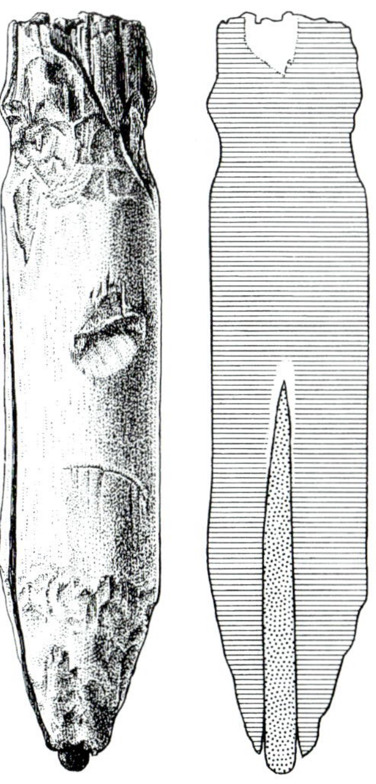

The net

In the course of the examinations of the site the remains of a net were recovered to the west of the stone slab on which the body lay. The rough mesh was made of lengths of grass and the net was probably used to catch birds.

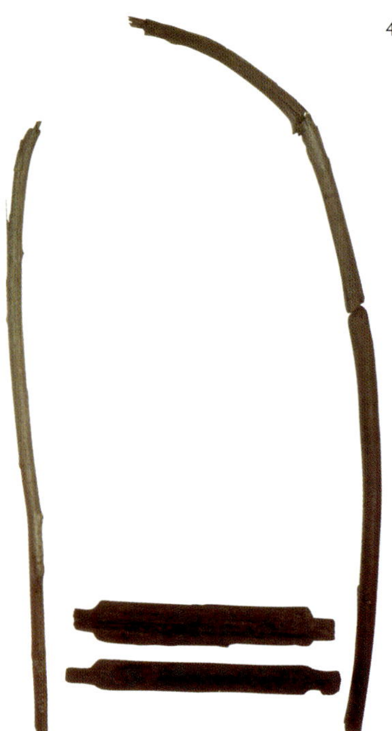

An exact reconstruction of the backpack is no longer possible

The backpack

A number of pieces of wood were found deposited on a rocky ledge along with the axe and bow. These included a 1.98 m hazel rod bent into a U-shape and two narrow wooden slats measuring respectively 38 and 40.3 cm made of larch-wood. The ends of the slats are worked into tongues or two notches. The ends of the hazel rod also each have two notches, one above the other. This suggests that the two wooden slats acted as horizontal links for the U-shaped hazelnut rod. The slats were tied together with grass string; various corresponding remains were found in the immediate vicinity. They consist of two twisted grass stalks. The pieces of wood form the frame of a backpack. Numerous bits of hide and clumps of hair suggest that a skin bag was fastened onto the carrying frame. The backpack lay higher up in the gully and therefore emerged from the melting snow sooner than the body. The objects deposited on this exposed ledge were laid open to the effects of sun and wind which also explains the deteriorated condition of the pack.

The Iceman carried altogether 18 different types of wood. He used the most appropriate type of wood for each tool. The man had a wide knowledge of the natural resources at his disposal and how best to use them.

The birch-bark containers

A birch-bark container was found right next to the dead man. The remains of a further container out of birch-bark was found near the backpack. Both are cylindrical in form. The slightly oval bottom measuring approximately 15–18 cm was made separately and attached to the vertical part. The nearly 20 cm high container is made of a rectangular piece of bark. This was rolled up and, as a row of holes indicates, sewn up on the side. The underside and the bottom also have a series of holes

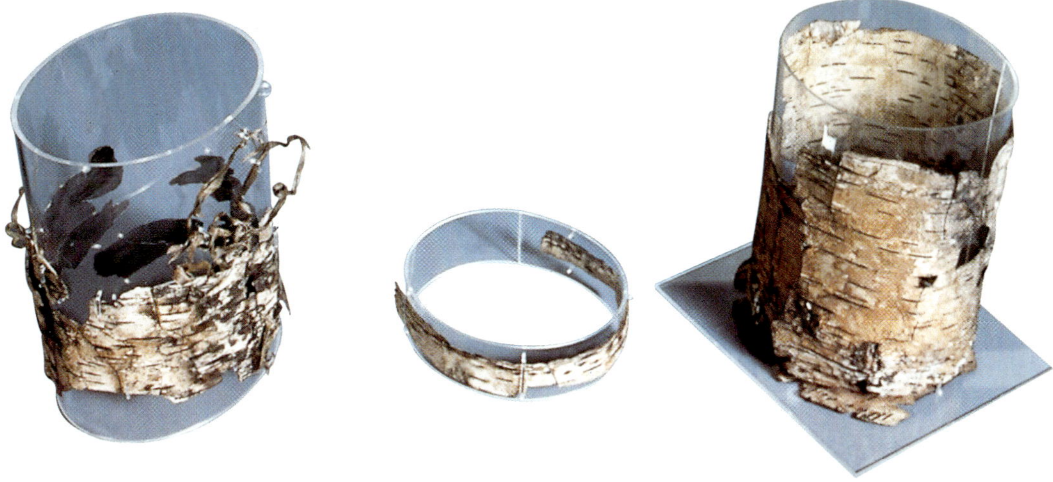

and were sewn together. No traces of the sewing material remain. Whilst the inside of the container found in the vicinity of the backpack still had the light colour of birch-bark, the inside of the other container was blackened. Amongst the contents of this container were maple leaves and embedded in these, spruce and juniper needles. Einkorn and wheat particles were also found. The leaves contained tiny particles of charcoal. The contents of the container suggest that it was used to carry embers and that the leaves which had been gathered specially for this purpose served as insulating material.

The Iceman carried his provisions in two birch bark containers

The active ingredients of the birch fungus stop bleeding and act as a disinfectant

The stone bead is the only piece of jewellery found

The birch fungus

Attached to his clothing, on two strips of hide, the Iceman carried spherical forms made of the flesh of the birch fungus. They served a medicinal purpose. Tree fungi were used right up into the 20th century for healing.

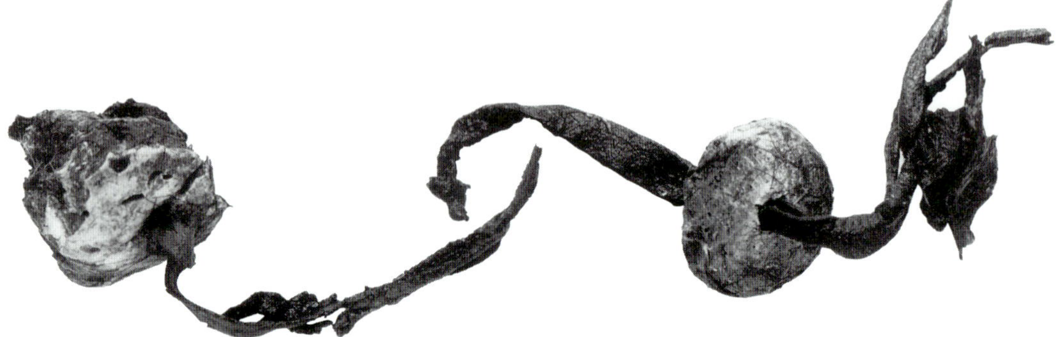

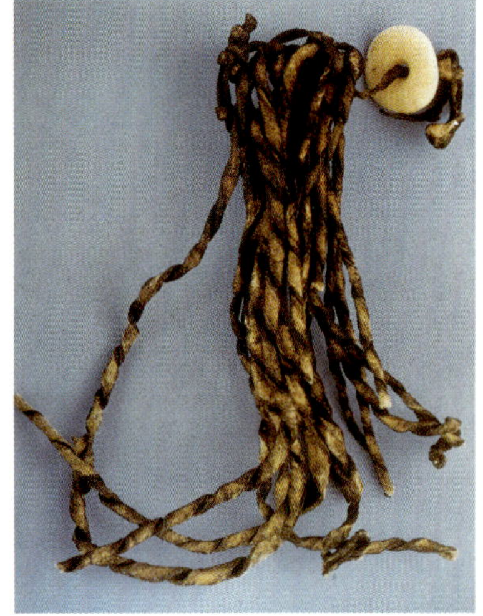

The tassel with the stone bead

The only object in the Iceman's gear which can be described as an adornment is a round marble bead. The bead has a hole through the middle and is threaded onto a thong. This holds together a bundle of strips twisted into a spiral which together form a sort of tassel. The hide strip is both decoration and spare parts or repair material.

The food remains

The food remains include a sloe berry and, in addition to the remains of grains in the birch-bark containers, two whole grains were found embedded in the fur of the clothing. They were einkorn. Although the grains may not have belonged to the provisions he took with him but arrived accidentally at the Tisenjoch, they prove that the man at least had contact with farming tribes in the valley. In the course of the examination of the site, two small bone splinters were found. The anatomical and zoological analyses showed that these belonged to the neck vertebra of an ibex. The Iceman had probably taken smoked or dried ibex meat with him on his journey.

The last meal

The contents of the large intestine of the Iceman were analysed at the Botanical Institute of the University of Innsbruck. According to the results, his last meal had consisted of a gruel made of einkorn, meat and unidentifiable plants. The grain was ground and could therefore have also been eaten in the form of bread. Mixed in traces of charcoal and minerals are partly responsible for the pronounced abrasion of the teeth. As the discovery of the sloe indicates, the man also gathered fruits with which he complemented his diet. Analysis of his large intestine showed that the man had suffered from nematodes when he was alive. Most informative for the research was the tree pollen and the small amount of plant pollen which was also discovered. Pollen can be absorbed both through food and through water and the air. Pollen from the following plants was identified: meadow grasses, plantain, beech, hazel, spruce. The types of tree indicate a typical mixed forest as found in the Val Venosta and in particular in the Senales valley. The pollen of the beech-tree, which only grows south of the Alps and therefore in the Val Venosta, provides an important clue as to where the Iceman came from. On account of the stage of digestion of the pollen, botanists conclude that the Iceman was in the Val Venosta 12 hours before his death. The other finds are also of particular importance in this respect because they provide information on the origin of the different types of wood. The pieces of wood give conclusive evidence on

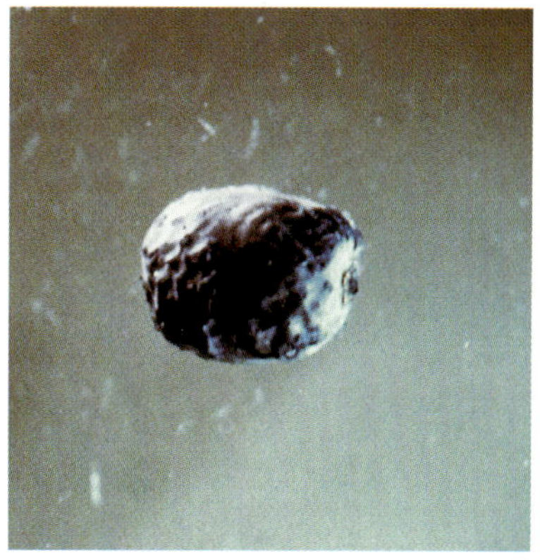

A sloe proves that the Iceman supplemented his diet with berries

his living environment. The spruce and oak forests in particular suggest steep inclines, mild winters and hot summers. These conditions are typical of the Val Venosta. Even the yew, out of which the bow-stave and the axe handle were made, used to be native to the Val Venosta.

The time of death

On the basis of the pollen, the time of death of the Iceman can be fairly accurately determined: the flowering season of the beech ends in June, the sloe, however, can be harvested between July and November. The man carried two maple leaves as insulating material with him in the ember-carrier. Their chlorophyll content shows that they were freshly picked and their stalks removed. They were harvested between June and September so we can conclude that the man died in spring or in early summer.

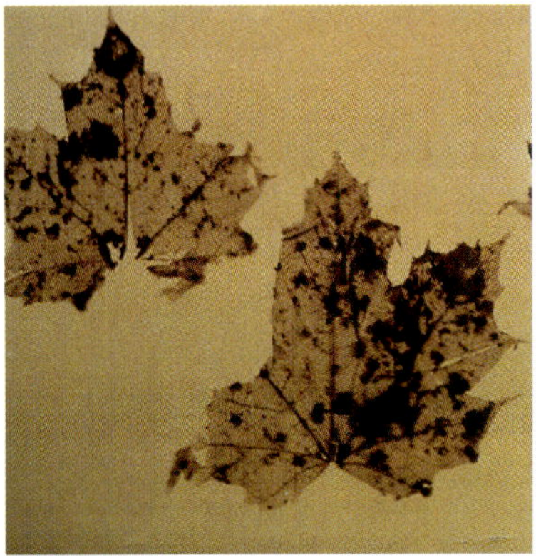

The maple leaves found in the birch bark containers bear traces of charcoal

Cultural origin

The find is absolutely unique and it is hard to determine its cultural origin. The absence of any pottery makes the attempt particularly difficult. Links can be made between the organic objects and late Neolithic and early Bronze Age pile-dwellings but on account of the fact that the organic materials were preserved in wetland environments this comparison loses its significance. In addition, research on Copper Age settlements in the central Alpine arc is relatively scant. From the middle Neolithic Age onwards, the Val Venosta can be associated with the "vasi a bocca quadrata" (Square-Mouthed Pottery Culture) which also played a role in the early Neolithic Period. It is not yet known to what extent the Remedello Culture, endogenous to the southern Alpine rim and the Lombard Alps, also played a role in the central Alpine region. The Tisenjoch axe does indeed correspond to the copper axes of the grave finds in the area after which the culture was named, Remedello near Brescia. In particular, the finds of the Remedello grave 102 can be compared to the equipment of the Iceman. A copper axe, a flint dagger and stemmed arrow-heads were found in the man's grave in Remedello. The spreading of the Remedello Culture into what is now South Tyrol can moreover be proved by the discovery of a number of flint daggers and flat copper axes. Surrounding cultural groups worth naming are the Horgen Culture in Switzerland and the Baden Culture in eastern Austria. The Altheim and Cham Cultures whose influence reached as far as the Inn valley in the Tyrol were predominant in Bavaria. In relation to the Iceman, another group of sources is of particular importance: the so-called statue stele which were widespread in the southern Alpine region. These also provided the first pictorial representations of, for example, axes, daggers and bows and arrows. The form of the daggers clearly replicates the so-called copper Remedello daggers. Moreover, a link can be made between these pictures of axes and the copper axes such as the one carried by the Iceman. The stones with pictures on them were probably related to the cult of the ancestors. The images show the

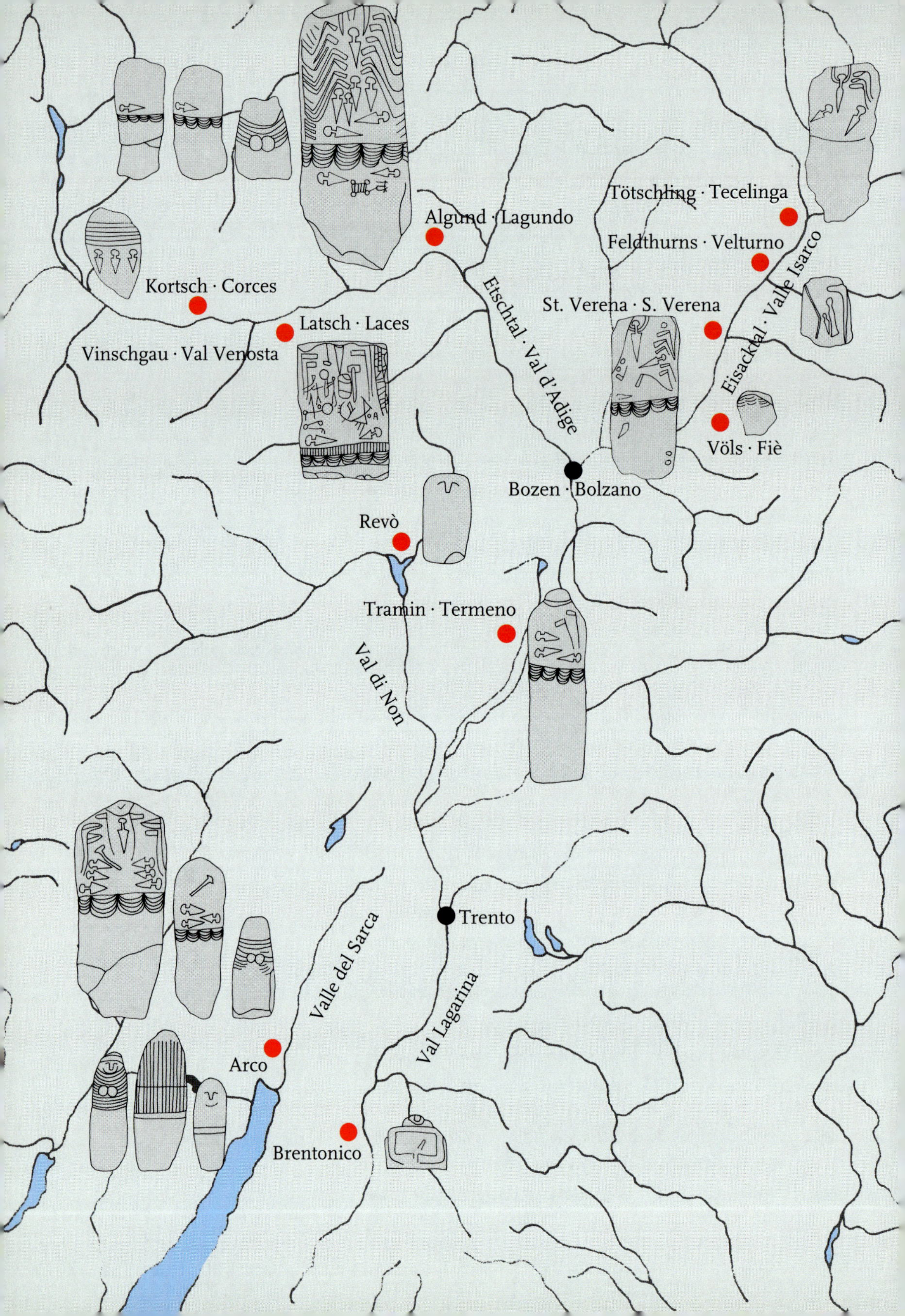

Tötschling · Tecelinga
Algund · Lagundo
Feldthurns · Velturno
Kortsch · Corces
St. Verena · S. Verena
Latsch · Laces
Etschtal · Val d'Adige
Eisacktal · Valle Isarco
Vinschgau · Val Venosta
Völs · Fiè
Bozen · Bolzano
Revò
Tramin · Termeno
Val di Non
Trento
Valle del Sarca
Val Lagarina
Arco
Brentonico

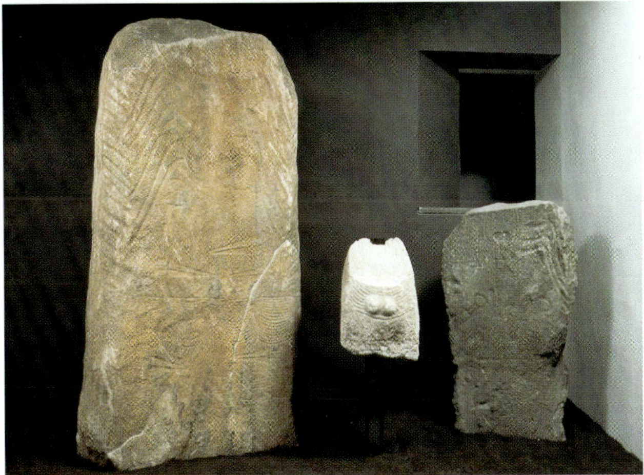

Map of the location of the statue stele in Trentino, South Tyrol

Male and female statue stele from Lagundo and from Tezzelinga

Drawing of the big statue stele from Lagundo

first achievements and products out of metal and give insight into cult aspects and into the social organisation and the fashion of the civilisation at the time. Metal objects were characteristic of the upper and ruling classes, as we can see in the pictures on the statue stele. A brooch and a breastplate of silver have also been identified as belonging to the Remedello Culture. In both burials and in representations on the stone statue stele, axes and daggers appear in connection with the upper classes. On account of his axe, the Iceman can probably be classed as a cattle owner or village chief or something similar. Hunting, searching for ore etc. also belonged to his range of activities as the bow and arrow indicate.

On the back of the statue stele, vertical, partly transposed grooves descend as far as the gathered, garland-like belt. These remind one of the Iceman's upper garment which consisted of vertical strips of skin sewn together.

The link between the Tisenjoch find and the Ötztal pasture-lands which, then as now were tended from the Val Venosta, should be mentioned. The man's gear, in particular the birch-bark containers, allows us to assume that he was equipped for a longer stay. The building of a fire also suggests a stay of a number of days away from a settlement. In the near vicinity of the Hauslabjoch, on the Rofenberg, analysis of pollen samples from 2,760 m above sealevel proved that the Alpine pastures were subject to human

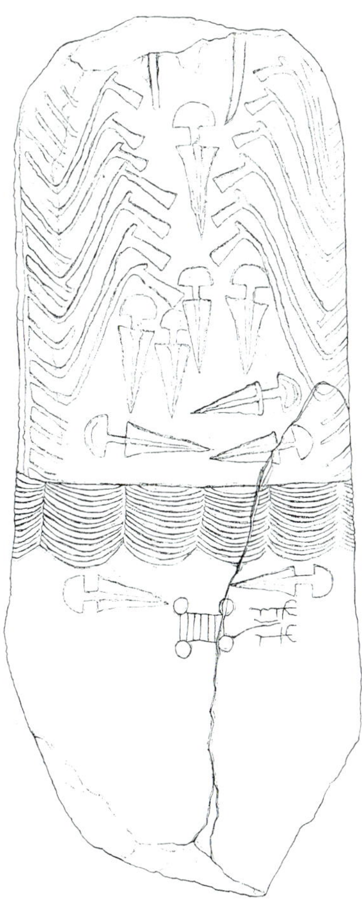

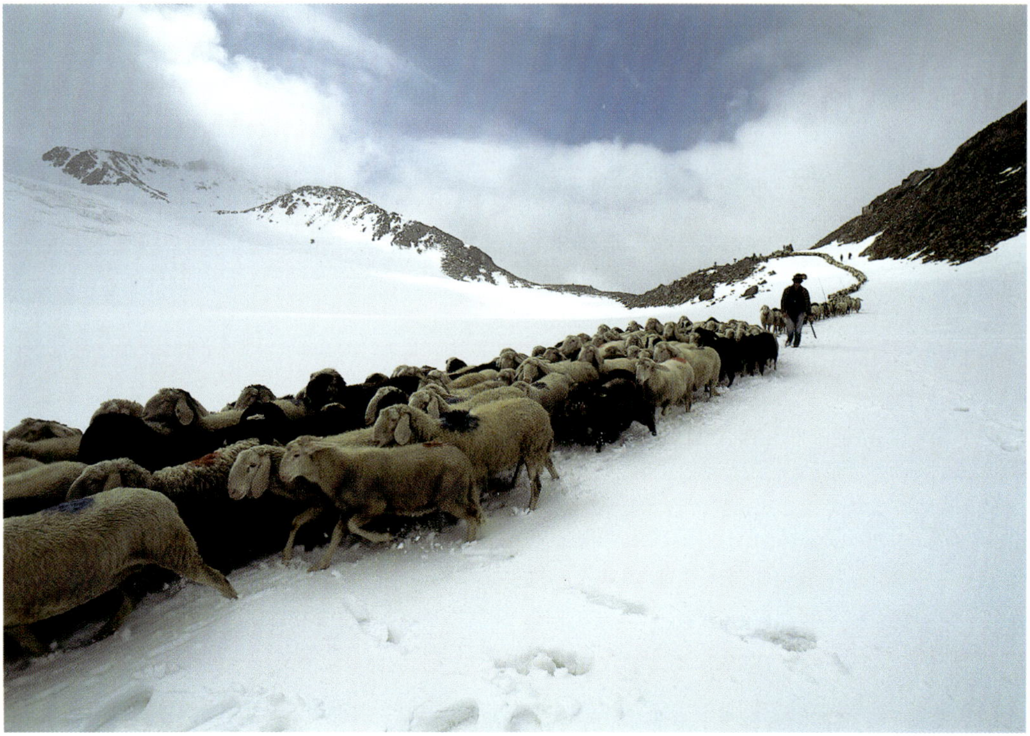

Driving the sheep from Senales to the Ötztal
The long ascent through the Tisental

The Senales Valley with the Similaunspitze (summit) in the background and Juval castle in the foreground

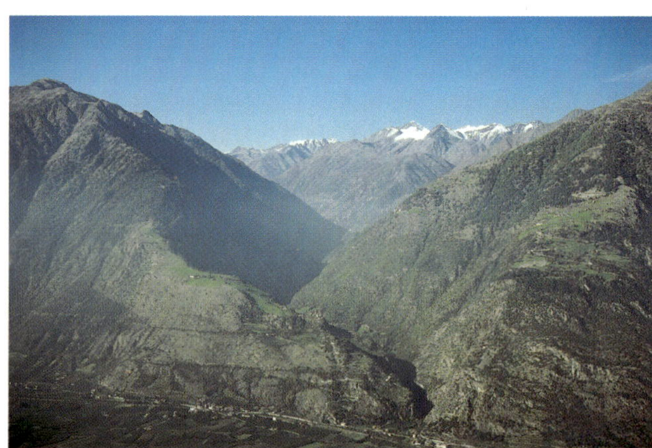

influence through stock-farming as early as the 4th millennium B.C. A change in the vegetation from heath-land with dwarf bushes to meadows with a wide variety of herbaceous plants has been established. The timberline was at 2,200–2,300 m above sealevel. The acreage above the treeline was artificially extended towards the valley. It can be assumed that the man lived in the Val Venosta. Neolithic and Bronze Age finds came to light in the extensive examination of the sites on the hill on which the castle of Juval is situated. It is possible that his home was here. The grain with which the Iceman came into contact was grown in the area around this settlement.

The return of the Iceman to the South Tyrol

On 16th January 1998, under the strictest security measures, the Iceman and the other finds were transported back from the Institute of Anatomy of the University of Innsbruck to the South Tyrol Museum of Archaeology in Bolzano. In its 1,200 m^2 of exhibition space, the new South Tyrol Museum of Archaeology documents the entire ancient and early history of the South Tyrol from the ancient and middle Stone Age up until the Carolingian Age. The mummy and the accompanying finds are of central importance and accordingly occupy the whole of the first floor of the museum.

The mummy being put into the cold-storage van

The convoy arriving on the Brenner Pass

Arriving at the South Tyrol Museum of Archaeology in Bolzano

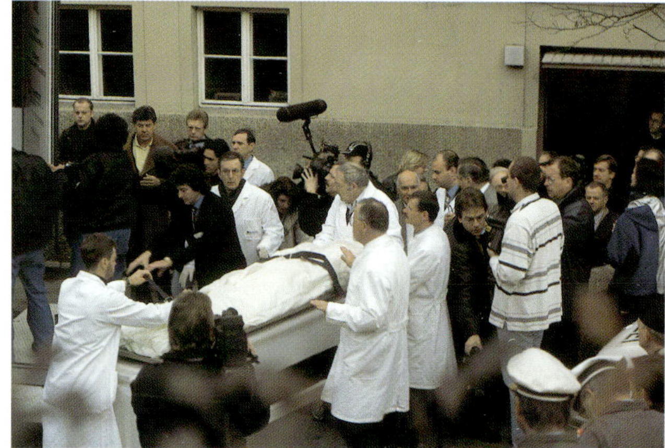

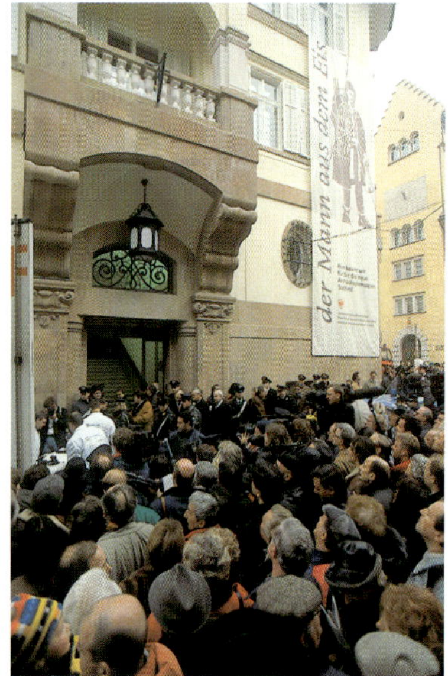

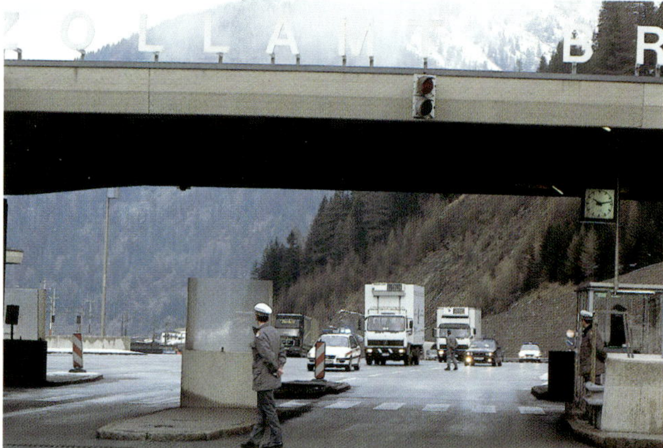

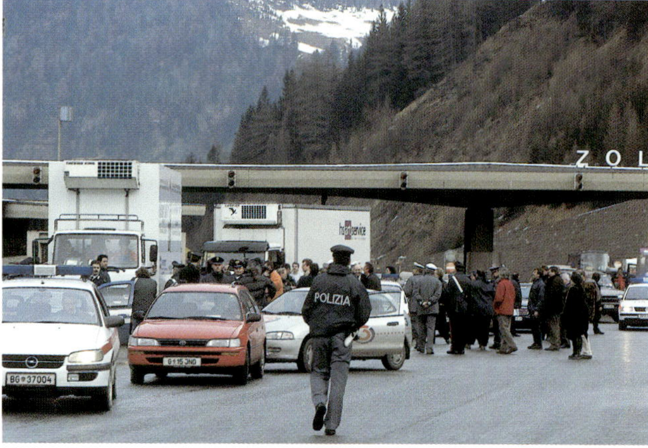

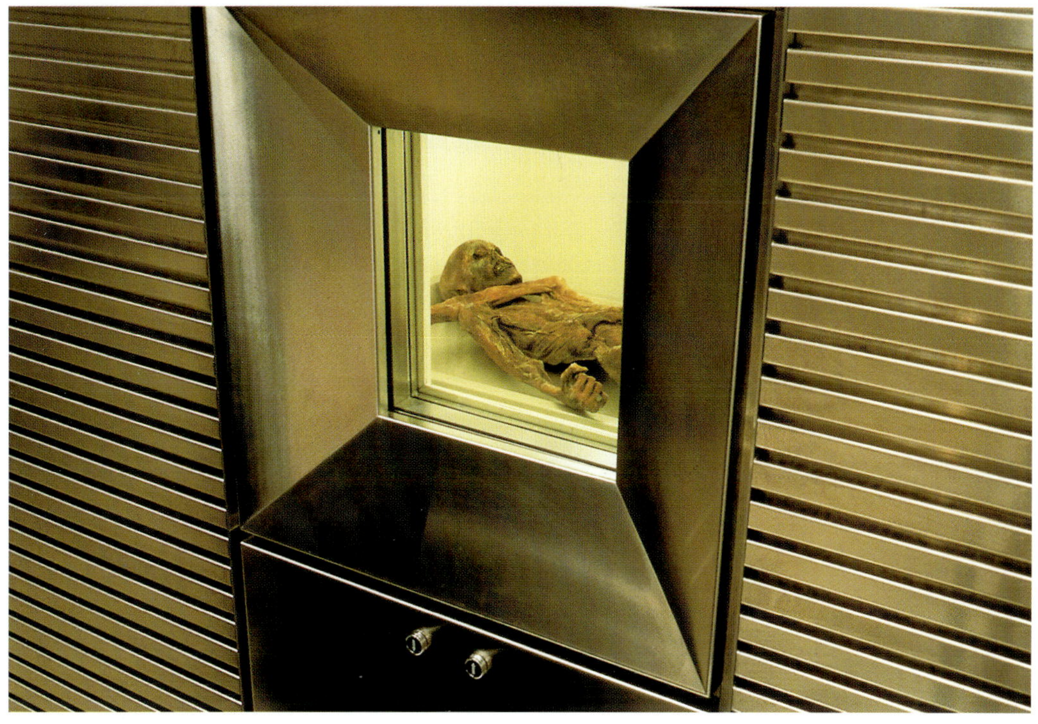

The view through the window into the cold chamber

Conservation in Bolzano

At the South Tyrol Museum of Archaeology the mummy is kept in a specially made cold store which is closed to the general public. The "Iceman box" consists of a decontamination room, an examination room and two adjoining identical refrigeration chambers with independent cooling systems. The mummy is kept in one of the chambers at – 6 °C and with an air humidity of almost 100 %. A complex global thermal system allows a controllable transfer of humidity between the cooling system and the mummy without ice forming on the body. It is thus no longer necessary to keep the body in crushed ice.

The problem with the lighting was solved through a special process in which a special filter removes the ultraviolet and infrared rays from the cold light. This also makes it possible for the public to view the mummy through a little window.

Bibliography

Konrad Spindler/Elisabeth Rastbichler-Zissernig/Harald Wilfing Dieter zur Nedden/Hans Nothdurfter (Hrsg.): Der Mann im Eis. Neue Funde und Ergebnisse. The Man in the Ice. Vol. 2 (= Veröffentlichungen des Forschungsinstituts für Alpine Vorzeit der Universität Innsbruck 2). Wien/New York 1995

Frank Höpfel/Werner Platzer/Konrad Spindler (Hrsg.): Der Mann im Eis. In: Der Mann im Eis. Bericht über das Internationale Symposium 1992 in Innsbruck. Vol. 1. (= Veröffentlichungen der Universität. Innsbruck, 187). Innsbruc 1992

Markus Egg/Roswitha Goedeeker-Ciolek/Willy Groenman van Waateringe/Konrad Spindler: Die Gletschermumie vom Ende der Steinzeit aus den Ötztaler Alpen. In: Jahrbuch des Römisch-Germanischen Zentralmuseums Mainz, 39 (1992), 1–128. Mainz 1993

Konrad Spindler: Der Mann im Eis. Die Ötztaler Mumie verrät d Geheimnisse der Steinzeit. München: Bertelsmann 1993

Picture credits

Lorenzo Dal Ri, South Tyrol Museum of Archaeology: 17
Gruppe Gut: 35, 48
Landesgendarmeriekommando für Tirol: 7, 10, 11 top, 22 top
Andreas Lippert: 16 top + bottom right
Werner Nosko: 13
Hans Nothdurfter, South Tyrol Museum of Archaeology: 16 left
Klaus Oeggl, University of Innsbruck: 45, 46
Josef Pernter: front cover, 5, 6, 27, 28 top, 29, 31 top, 32 right, 33, 39 top, 40 top, 41 top, 43, 49 top, 53, 55
Römisch-Germanisches Zentralmuseum Mainz: front cover, front flap, 3, 22 bottom, 28 bottom, 30bottom, 31 bottom, 36, 37 top right + bottom, 38 left, 39 bottom, 40 bottom, 41 bottom, 42, 44
Marco Samadelli: 9, 30 top, 37 top left, 38 top right, 50 bottom
Max Scherer, Vienna Report: 12 top + middle, 14 top + bottom, 18
Othmar Seehauser: back cover, 15, 32 bottom left, 50 top, 52
Sara Welponer: 26, 32 left, 34, 35, 49 bottom
University of Innsbruck: 12 bottom
Uno Press: 11 bottom, 12 middle left
Dieter zur Nedden, University of Innsbruck: 19, 20.

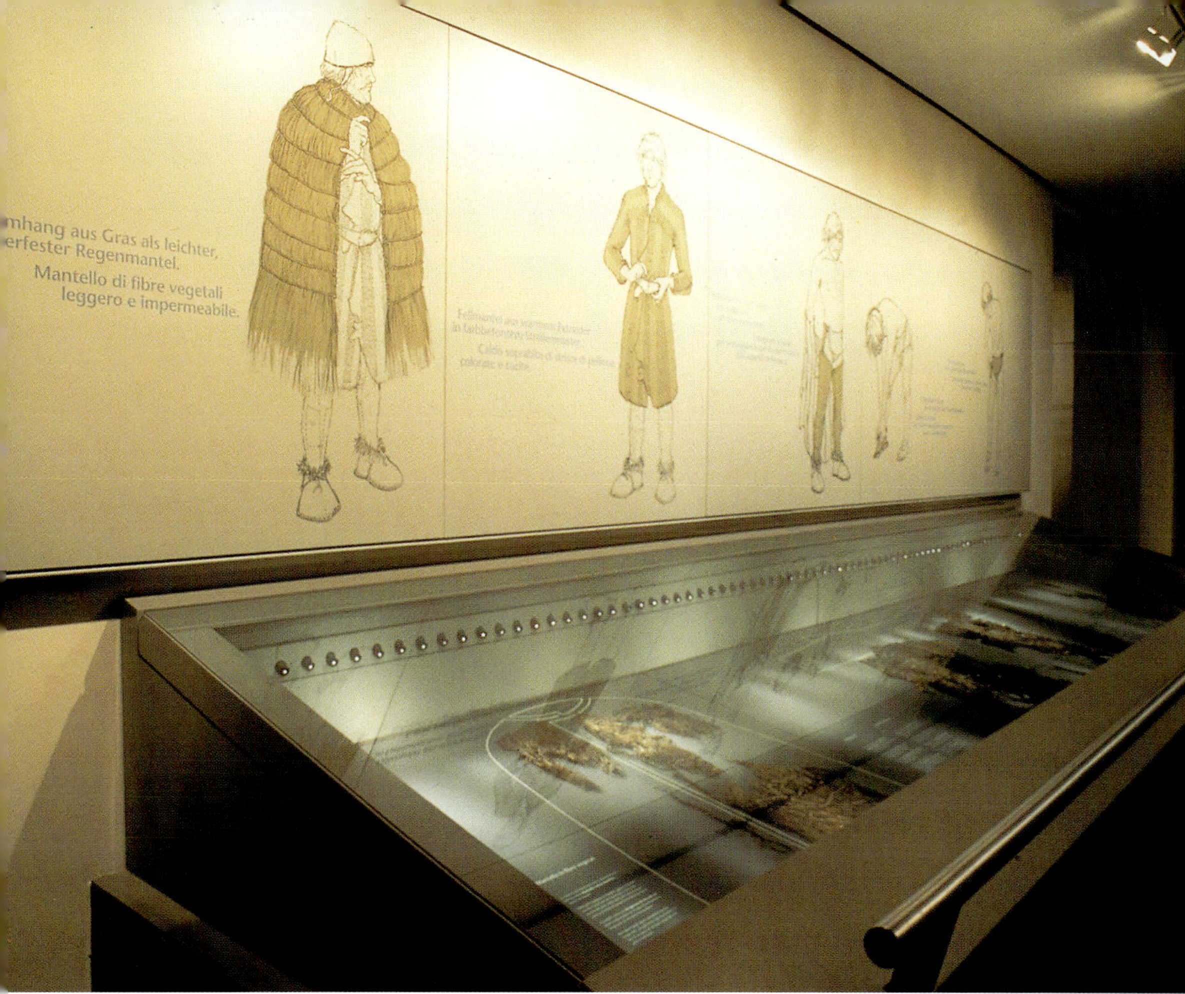

The exhibition space with the other Iceman findings on the first floor of the South Tyrol Museum of Archaeology